DATE DUE

WOMEN AT WORK IN THE GULF

K

WOMEN AT WORK IN THE GULF

A Case Study of Bahrain

MUNIRA A. FAKHRO

KEGAN PAUL INTERNATIONAL
London and New York

land

Distributed by
John Wiley & Sons Ltd
Southern Cross Trading Estate
1 Oldlands Way, Bognor Regis
West Sussex, PO22 9SA, England

Routledge, Chapman & Hall Inc
29 West 35th Street
New York, NY 10001, USA

The Canterbury Press Pty Ltd
Unit 2, 71 Rushdale Street
Scoresby, Victoria 3179, Australia

Set in Times
by Columns Design and Production Services Ltd

Printed in Great Britain by
T. J. Press Ltd

British Library Cataloguing in Publication Data

Fakhro, Munira A. (Munira Ahmed), 1941
Women at work in the gulf: a case study of Bahrain.
1. Arab countries. Women personnel
I. Title
331.4'0917'4927

ISBN 0–7103–0337–8

US Library of Congress Cataloging in Publication Data
Applied for

To my two sons: Ayad and Talal Algosaibi

Contents

List of Tables

List of Maps

Preface

This book grew out of a dissertation written during 1983–86 and is an analysis of the social policies needed to facilitate women's entry into the labour force.

It is essential now for Gulf women to move beyond their domestic activities by taking an active role and by providing leadership to ensure that they have access to the opportunities and benefits of economic development.

While the study was slowly taking shape I made a number of trips to different international agencies including the ILO in Geneva, UNESCO and the OECD in Paris. Such trips enabled me to make fruitful contacts with a number of officials and specialists who provided information on vocational training, literacy programs and the European experience with foreign labour.

The tables presented here are entirely new in the sense that data were selected from 1941–81 censuses. Other statistics were drawn from different sources reflecting developments during the 1980s.

Finally I would like to express my deepest appreciation to all those who helped me. I am particularly grateful to my adviser Dr Alfred Kahn of Columbia University for his valuable comments and constructive criticism.

Bahrain, June 1989

Preface

Chapter One

Introduction

Demographic Characteristics of the Population in Bahrain

According to the 1981 census, the total population of Bahrain is 350,798; the employed population – 15 years old and over – is estimated at 146,133. Statistics regarding women in the labor force show that only 12,176 of Bahraini females, or 8.3% of the total, are in the labour force. The number of Bahraini males in the labor force is 52,400 (35.9%), whereas the rest of the labor force (81,497 or 55.8%) is made up of foreigners. In the private sector, the proportion of foreign workers is much higher than their proportion in the public sector. In 1982, the percentage of Bahraini employees who worked in the private sector comprised 25.7%, whereas the non-Bahrainis made up 74.3% of the labor force.

The heavy reliance upon immigrant labor is related to the boom of the post-oil economic infrastructure that increased sharply after 1973. The government of Bahrain, as well as the governments of other Gulf states, responded to the manpower shortage by allowing the market forces to rule. Labor was imported with little official constraint; the result was an overflow of workers of massive proportion.[1]

In 1975, the number of foreign workers in Bahrain was 29,100. That number has been increasing over the years. The World Bank study (1983) predicted that with high growth rates in 1985, there would be about 81,400 foreign workers in Bahrain.[2] However, the 1981 census revealed this growth projection had been realized in 1981, four years earlier than predicted. The 1981 census showed also that the foreign population as a whole, counting spouses and dependents, had grown from 37,990 in 1971 to 112,400 in 1981, an increase of 197% in only one decade. Moreover, the population is expected to reach three-quarters of a million in the year 2000 (463,357 Bahrainis and 286,733 non-Bahrainis). This rapid growth rate of foreign population from 18% in 1971 to 32% in 1981 reflects the magnitude of the problem of the rapidly increasing size of the foreign population in Bahrain as well as in the other Gulf states where foreign population exceeds 75% of the total. Crude participation rates (the percentage of the population that works) is estimated to range from 18.5% in Qatar, 19% in Kuwait to 24.9% in Oman. In Bahrain, the crude participation rate was 21.3%,[3] still an alarming rate compared to the rate in some industrial countries. In France, Germany and Switzerland, for example, foreign workers formed 10.9%, 9.7% and 12.8% respectively of the economically active population of those countries in 1976; this relatively small percentage was considered a very serious problem and different measures have been taken to minimize the threat posed by the foreign workers.

The workforce in the Gulf states is even smaller than would be expected from a total population of this size. This phenomenon is related to three factors:[4]

1. The population of the Gulf states is very young: of Qatar's small population of 68,000, over 44% are less than 15 years old. This phenomenon can be seen more clearly in Bahrain, where the Bahraini population numbers 238,420; nearly 129,760 or 54.5% are 19 years and under.
2. The widespread expansion of secondary and university education during the 1970s had held within the educational system boys and girls who otherwise would have entered the workforce at a younger age. This factor reduces the labor force significantly.
3. The third factor is that the labor force is reduced by the limited number of females, who work mostly in occupations such as teaching, nursing or secretarial jobs and in some women's organizations.

Yet, despite this limited size of an indigenous workforce, the Gulf states have embarked upon economic development and industrialization. The 1973 oil-price boom enabled the Gulf states to invest in industry and to build the infrastructure, but the major obstacle to this economic development was the shortage of manpower, which was seen by planners as the major constraint to development.

HISTORICAL BACKGROUND

Most studies of international labor migration in the Gulf States have emphasized the period since the 1973 oil price increase. However, foreign laborers were imported to the Gulf a long time ago, even prior to oil discovery.

The existence of foreign labor in Bahrain can be traced back to the discovery of oil in 1932, when there was a great demand for skilled labor. The increasing immigration of Persians had begun to cause concern in 1937. Belgrave (the British adviser to the ruler of Bahrain) requested the Bahraini Petroleum Company (BAPCO) not to employ non-Bahraini workers.[5] However, the number of Persians employed increased from 429 (March 1937) to 555 (September 1937), whereas the number of Indian nationals registered in Bahrain had grown from 450 in 1930 to 1550 in 1938. In 1948, complaints were made to the Bahraini government about the number of foreigners, particularly Indians, Pakistanis and Persians who were employed in Bahrain at the expense of local labor.[6] Thus the recent growth of immigration from the Indian sub-continent is not a new phenomenon but 'the recrudescence of a tradition of migration dating back to the 1930s and encouraged by the rapid exhaustion of Arab labor supplies'.[7]

However, since 1973, the flow of foreign labor has increased dramatically. In 1971, foreign labor in Bahrain formed 37% of the total labor force, but the real expansion of foreign labor had started in 1973 and increased in 1976 to reach a total of 30,180 or 39.2% of the total labor force. Bahraini workers reached nearly 47,000. In 1971, the Asian foreign labor increased to 27% of the total labor force and reached 65% in 1977, whereas the Arab labor force decreased from 54% in 1971 to 16% in 1977.[8] Many Arab workers were being replaced by Asians. Asian workers are considered to be less of a threat to the stability of the local societies of the Gulf states because they share few cultural ties with the nationals.

The 1975 statistics showed that the percentage of Arab workers was 20% of the total foreign workers; the Asian workers formed

55.3%, whereas European workers showed a lower percentage of 14.7%. As for other Gulf states, the problem is even more critical. Foreigners in Kuwait, Qatar and UAE comprise over half the residents; 35% are non-Arabs. The number of foreign workers in the Gulf states was expected to rise from 1.3 million in 1975 to 2.8 million in 1985, and the increase of south-east Asians was expected to be sharp.[9]

FACTORS AFFECTING THE DECLINE IN NATIONAL MANPOWER

Government polices in Bahrain, as well as in the other Gulf states, concerning migration and population policies are completely absent. In other words, the absence of such a policy is in itself a policy. The government of Bahrain is reluctant to formulate migration policies. It fears that foreign workers would become organized to the extent that they would demand better living conditions and higher salaries. In every way possible, the government wants to limit the power of foreign workers so that they can be controlled. The government has diversified foreign labor nationalities in order to prevent one group from becoming a strong power. One strategy is to increase the number of Asians, who are cheaper to employ and who contribute less to the political pressures on the government. At the same time, the government is likely to keep the proportion of the national labor force as small as possible in order to control it.

Inadequacy in the educational system is another factor contributing to the decline in national manpower. Although public schools in Bahrain were founded in 1919, earlier than in any other Gulf states, they are considered inefficient and inadequate. The high rate of repeaters and drop-outs, from which public education in Bahrain suffers, is related to such inefficiency. Also it is of importance that the curriculum does not fulfill the requirements of labor demands in cases where there is a lack of coordination between education and manpower requirements. At the same time, job classification does not fit within the education training.[10] Most educational systems in the Gulf states today can be characterized as heavily biased toward the arts and literature, with university education at the top of the educational pyramid. Moreover, courses are essentially repetitive; the same blend of subjects is studied at all educational levels. At the secondary level, little variation is introduced to allow students to choose arts or sciences. In sum, the educational system is not well adapted to the needs of modern economic development.[11]

One major problem is that compulsory education has not yet been introduced. One can relate the high percentage of illiteracy, especially among females, to the absence of a compulsory education law. The 1981 census showed that the percentage of illiterates in Bahrain's total population was 25.2% for males and 48.1% for females. The percentage of illiterate females is even higher among people 10 to 44 years of age. In this age group, there are 26,724 illiterate persons: 6,218 males and 20,506 females.

Lack of efficient training programs is another major factor contributing to the decline in national manpower. In Bahrain, as well as in many Arab countries, manual work is given a lower status than white collar jobs. The World Bank study predicts that the future supply of manpower in the Gulf states will be 8% from university liberal arts courses and only 3% from vocational or secondary technical courses. Such a low percentage of national manpower does not serve the labor market's demands well.[12]

UNDER-EMPLOYMENT AMONG FEMALE NATIONALS

It is a general belief that economic necessity is a major reason for a job search. But in the case of females in Bahrain, the situation is more complicated. Besides becoming economically independent, educated women are seeking an active role in society. As mentioned earlier, Bahraini women constitute nearly 8.3% of the overall labor force. Most working women are employed at different government agencies, where very few hold administrative positions. The majority work as secretaries and clerks.

Under-employment among female nationals could be related to social, cultural and political barriers. Such barriers keep most females away from joining the labor force. National manpower supplies in the Gulf states are limited in the main because most nationals entering the labor force do not have the proper educational qualifications. Furthermore, the demographic structure of the population makes overall male participation low.[13] Thus, employing more females would be preferable because the participation rate of nationals in the labor force would increase.

However, the most important barrier that keeps more women from joining the labor force is their educational level. Different

Table 1.1 *Employed Bahraini persons in the private sector by sex and educational level, 1982*

	Male	Female	Total
1. Illiterate	3,164	71	3,235
2. Not Illiterate	16,564	3,460	18,953
Total	19,728	3,531	22,188

Sources: Annual statistics for 1982, derived from Table 6, *Employment in the Private Sector by Educational Level, 1982*, Ministry of Labor and Social Affairs (Arabic).

studies have shown a substantial relationship between female education and female employment. The higher the woman's level of education, the greater the woman's employability. The high participation rates displayed by university-educated women in Moslem countries indicate a strong demand for professional and technical services and a positive response by highly educated women to meet this demand.[14]

Such correlation between female education and female employment is observed among working females in Bahrain. Table 1.1 shows that the total number of illiterate females who worked in the private sector was 71 whereas those who had acquired some degree of education numbered 3,460; this means that only 2% of females who worked in the private sector were illiterate. As for the public sector, the percentage was relatively higher than that of the private sector. The 1981 census showed that their number was only 523 or 7.8% of the total females working in the public sector. This small percentage of working illiterate females indicates that education forms a crucial factor in integrating more women into the labor force.

Another barrier that keeps more females from joining the labor force is the inadequacy of existing vocational training programmes. Such programmes cannot respond effectively to labor market demands. Females are not allowed to join such programs as electrical or mechanical engineering or management, which are considered as 'men's jobs'. Instead, females are encouraged to join such programs as sewing and hair styling. Such programs have proved to be less successful because they have not been linked to market demand and therefore have not offered a steady income for those who joined them.

Another important barrier that limits women's employment is the inefficiency of child care services. Working mothers with young children entered the labor force before there were adequate and efficient child care facilities. The absence of such services made it more difficult for them to continue working, and most of them were forced to quit their jobs in order to stay at home and care for their children.

Day care centers and nurseries in Bahrain are few, inadequate and inefficient. In 1975–76, the number of such facilities was 8 day care centers and nurseries and the number of children enrolled was 815. In 1981–82, the number increased to 16 day care centres and nurseries, whereas the number of children enrolled increased to 2,003; this meant that only 5% of the population aged (0–4) was using such facilities. However, in 1985/86 the number increased to 64 with 5,000 children under 6 years of age enrolled.

Traditional Islamic laws concerning women and family could be considered as major barriers to women's integration in the labor force. In Bahrain and in the rest of the Gulf states, the classical, traditional Islamic law (Shari'a) is strictly observed. Under such law, women still suffer from child marriage, polygamy, the guardian's right to contract marriage and, moreover, men continue to enjoy the right to unilateral divorce, to have custody of the children and to benefit from the bias in the inheritance laws that specify that men inherit twice as much as women. Reforms that reduce the inequalities in traditional Islamic law affecting women are an essential aspect of the process of social development. Without such reforms, a high literacy rate, a low birth rate and a high participation of women in the labor force (characteristics of economic and social development) are not likey to happen.

Dimensions of Foreign Labor Increase

The increase of foreign labor is as great as its impact. The fear is that as nationals become a minority, their national identity and culture will be lost. Superficially, one can notice how foreigners have brought with them many foreign words, mostly English and Indian. On a more substantial level, the population in each Gulf state increased from 4 to 20 times from 1960–80, and cultural changes have led to an increase in housing problems and in crime rates.[15]

Political costs should be considered if foreign workers become citizens and begin to demand political rights. Moreover, as families of migrant workers travel to Bahrain and other Gulf states to join them, they become a more complete unit within the host country. With the establishment of nuclear family groups come political evolution and awareness. These groups become more concerned about securing rights similar to those enjoyed by the nationals for themselves and their children.[16]

As families continue to be brought to the country, there is a greater likelihood that the foreign population will receive citizenship, perhaps in a generation or so.

The European countries such as France and Germany in particular have already been faced with this experience and have encountered unsolvable dilemmas. Among these dilemmas are the economic costs. In Bahrain, for example, the transfer of money that is earned by foreigners and is then sent to their home state hurts Bahrain's budget. Although figures are not availabe for Bahrain, they do exist for the Gulf states. In 1981, workers from Pakistan alone who worked in the Gulf states sent home money to the value of $2 bn.

The living conditions of foreign workers are extremely inconvenient. Foreign workers, especially unskilled Asians, live in poor accommodation. Of all apartments in Bahrain 40% are ocupied by these workers. Collective housing (old stores and government housing) accommodates 3,108 families or 12.5% of the overall population. The Asian foreign workers form the majority of those who live in such facilities. Sometimes one old house with eight to ten rooms accommodates more than one hundred persons of different nationalities.[17]

Furthermore, each foreigner seeking employment should have a contract and a national sponsor (Kafil) as a prerequisite for obtaining a visa, a residence, and a work permit. Some sponsors may simply import labor and then retail it out to other local employers for a percentage of their wages. This person often keeps the passport and all traveling documents of those foreign workers whom he sponsors. Thus they cannot travel or leave the country or work for anyone else without his consent. The sponsor also has the right to terminate the employment of a sponsored person at will and can demand his deportation at any time.[18]

It can be said that foreign laborers, especially the unskilled, are given the worst housing; they feel socially and politically alienated and suffer from discrimination either by custom or by law. Such discrimination has become more severe in the last three years since the decrease in oil revenues. The laborers are either returned to their home countries or suffer abuse by employers, often their own compatriots.

The government of Bahrain has taken measures in order to minimize the threat of the increase of foreign workers; the most important one is to recruit unaccompanied males to build large industrial facilities. This enables the industrial areas to be operated like work camps with minimum services. This enclave arrangement would limit the mix and integration of foreign workers with the local work force. The Bahrain dry dock was the first contract of this type. The facilities for the Arab Shipbuilding and Repair Yard Company (ASRY) were built by Koreans under a $30 m contract. The labor force was made up entirely of Koreans. During the construction, they worked twelve-hour shifts to complete the project on time. They were self-sufficient in housing, food and recreational facilities. After the completion of the dock, the Korean workers left Bahrain.[19] Such work camps minimize the cultural impact of the expatriate labor force.

Recently, the government took new measures to minimize the foreign labor threat. A new registration system was introduced in 1984 whereby every individual living in Bahrain can be identified and coded. The government is trying to increase control beyond passport and visa identification, which in the case of contract labor could sometimes be falsified under the pre-existing system. The new measures will help by providing stricter accounting of those who live in and who pass through the country.[20]

The European Experience

One can draw some lessons from the experience of European countries in dealing with the migrant workers. In the early sixties when migrant workers came in large numbers to work in Europe, they were welcomed. In the mid-1970s, with the economic crisis and rising unemployment, the migrant question became a political issue, and the governments of Europe tried to place heavy restrictions on new immigrants.

In the following pages, the experience of West Germany, France and Sweden will be presented and examined in relation to the situation Bahrain and the other Gulf states are facing at present.

WEST GERMANY AND FRANCE

Immigrants from less-developed countries who live in Western Europe are estimated at twelve million. Many are trapped; their countries of origin cannot feed them and the host countries no longer want them.[21] In France the number of immigrants reached 1,680,500, and in West Germany, it exceeded 1,663,100. However, the attempt to substitute a national labor force for immigrant labor has largely been a failure. This is so because even in times of economic crisis and unemployment, there are certain jobs that nationals cannot perform. Moreover, for doing the most unpleasant work, immigrants are also paid less.[22]

A recent study by the city of Dusseldorf in West Germany showed that it is not in the benefit of the city if the foreigners quit their jobs; garbage would remain stinking on sidewalks, hospitals would not be able to cope and some schools would close down. In addition, the city would lose $3.6 m in pension contributions.[23] Moreover, drug abuse, prostitution and other crimes flourish in many immigrant ghettos; this is similar to what is happening in some parts of the Gulf states where some foreign workers smuggle drugs to the Gulf region.

In the meantime, racial tension is increasing in big cities in France, West Germany and Britain. In France, government demographers have predicted that within fifteen years, more than half of those under twenty-five in France will be of foreign origin. In 1976 in France and West Germany, the children of foreigners represented 9.7% and 16% of all live births respectively. Some experts view such high birth rates with alarm, fearing that in the long run, the second generation of guest workers will be the source of social and political unrest. Some observers feel that the children of guest workers who are educated in the labor host countries are unwilling to accept the low pay and low jobs previously sought so eagerly by their parents.[24]

The formation of guest-worker policies in Western Europe was considered a result of post-war economic expansion. Guest workers were initiated in spite of a public climate generally hostile to the idea of bringing in foreign workers, but because it was thought that these workers would be temporary and they could be sent home in the event of an economic down-turn, the idea of importing such a great number of foreign workers became acceptable.

Unlike Bahrain, and the Gulf states, where foreign workers are imported by local job agencies, the governments of France and West Germany controlled the importation of foreign workers. Employer requests for guest workers were processed by governmental agencies, which then recruited workers abroad. Through bilateral treaty arrangements, satellite offices were established in the countries in origin; guest workers were selected from lists of names submitted by labor officials in the country of recruitment. The transportation of the workers was arranged by the two governments as part of the fee paid by the employers.[25]

In West Germany, the guest-worker policy can be traced back to 1955 when several thousand Italian farm workers were granted temporary work permits. The German policy was predicated upon the notion that guest-worker employment should be a function of the labor market situation and economic conditions.

In 1970, German guest-worker policy changed after the realization that foreign workers were going to be a permanent work force. In 1973, the government decided to put more restrictions on guest workers' importation.

At present, unemployment in West Germany has reached 9.6%. The West German government has decided to encourage the Turks and other guest workers to return to their native country. Under the program that started in June 1984 and ended in September 1984, laid-off foreigners who left for their homelands could apply for a one-time bonus of $3,990, plus an additional $570 for each child. They were given their pension funds and one-way plane tickets. Nearly 55,000 guest workers, most of them Turks, applied for the program. It seems doubtful that Bahrain and the other Gulf states woud be able to take similar measures.

This situation was unlike the one in France, where permanent migration was to be officially encouraged because of the early decline in the French birth rate immediately after World War II. Different governmental agencies recommended that massive immigration be promoted as part of a long-term manpower and repopulation strategy. As industry expanded in the 1960s, new job opportunities were opened to foreign workers, and dependency on foreign workers for unskilled labor increased. With it came the social stigma that was attached to low-paid jobs, a situation which created more discrimination and racism.

As the number of guest workers increased, dependents abroad joined their families in host countries. After a year, the demand on social services increased. Soon, guest workers began to participate in political parties, trade unions and in their own autonomous political organizations.[26] However, in recent years, guest workers in France were often able to mobilize support to influence public affairs on their behalf.

It is true that guest-worker programs in West Germany and France have enabled the two countries to carry on their economic growth in the post-war period, but the long-term problems are numerous. One major problem is that the countries have become dependent upon foreign workers to provide manpower for key industry. Another problem is that foreign worker employment has tended to depress wages and to cause working conditions to deteriorate, especially with regard to unskilled labor. Furthermore, as foreign workers become long-term residents, they and their dependants require more social services and governmental infrastructure expenditures.

Guest workers in both countries remain non-citizens, despite having become an essential component of the work force. However, in recent years, European governments have been giving an increased importance to the foreign worker question. Many solutions were presented; one is their forced return to their countries of origin. Such forced returns may occur for instance in the case of the non-renewal of a contract or in the case of an offer of a certain amount of money made by the authorities of the host country to the worker if he returns home (as in the case of West Germany).

Such restrictive policies were formulated because doubts were raised about the desirability of hiring foreign workers. Those doubts were not so much of an economic nature as of a social nature. Frequently, foreign laborers lived in areas characterized very often by a lack of adequate housing facilities, recreation opportunities and other services such as schools, clinics and community centers. This situation was worsened by the inflow of foreign workers. Social tensions occurred between the local population and foreign workers, which sometimes resulted in violent clashes. Gradually it became clear that there was a limit to the absorption capacity of the local population as far as the integration and assimilation of the migrants was concerned. Economic doubts were gradually raised regarding the employment of such large numbers of foreign laborers. Such doubts were based on studies carried out in European host countries indicating that the net contribution that foreign workers make to the economy is outweighed by the costs involved for housing, training, health services and general guidance. Especially when a family came together, the additional costs required for the social and educational services made the employment of foreign labor disadvantageous from a macro-economic point of view.[27]

SWEDEN

It would be useful to study the experience of Sweden in dealing with the problem of manpower shortage. Because of the shortage of labor in the mid-1960s, Sweden faced an increasing demand to recruit more women in the labor market.

The labor unions were interested in keeping the level of immigration low. In the 1950s, labor shortages were common in most industrial countries. Many foreign workers were hired in such low-paid service industries as mines and factories. Most of these workers came to Europe from North Africa, Yugoslavia, Turkey and Greece. As for Sweden the majority of the foreign workers came from Finland and Yugoslavia.[28]

Sweden strongly rejected the guest worker (Gastarbeiter) system of the kind applied in West Germany and France. The main principle underlying the Swedish immigration policy is that immigrants are to be treated on an equal basis with Swedes. This means an expansion in new housing, schools and other services. Women at home, therefore, came to be regarded as an untapped labor supply.

The labor market policy has aimed both at keeping unemployment at a low level and at stimulating women to enter the labor force. The government's labor market policy has been concerned with helping women achieve a position in their working life equivalent to that of men, primarily by encouraging and easing their entry into the labor market.[29]

In the 1960s, Sweden turned instead to its own women. It appeared to be less expensive to induce Swedish women to reenter the labor force in different occupations than to continue assimilating masses of immigrants. The cost of immigrant labor was calculated not in terms of accommodations for male workers, who usually left their families in their homelands, but in terms of an infrastructure of housing, health services, schools, vocational training and language instruction – well beyond what most countries supplied to 'guest workers'.[30]

In 1972, the government appointed an advisory council on equality between men and women, which was responsible directly to the Prime Minister's office. The demand for equality involves changes not only in the conditions of women but also in the conditions of men. One purpose of such changes is to give women an increased opportunity for gainful employment and to give men an increased responsibility in the care of children.[31] In other words, to place women in 'male' jobs and to place men in 'female' ones is a way of trying to expand their choice of occupations, so that men and women will have a better chance to find jobs that fit them personally as individuals. Labor market policy has increased its efforts to break down sexual segregation in the labor market in order to create equal opportunity for men and women.

The main development since 1950 is that more and more married women have entered the labor market, many of whom have young children. In 1974, 57% of mothers with children under 7 years of age were gainfully employed.

Even during periods of economic recession, women have continued to increase their degree of participation in the labor force. In 1968 55% of all women aged 20–64 in Sweden had joined the labor force. By 1980, the corresponding figure increased to 75%. At this time there were more than 4 million people in the labor force (1.8 million women and nearly 2.3 million men) out of a total population of over 8 million.[32]

In 1972 a new family policy was adopted. It stresses that both parents should work outside the home. Family policy was seen as a tool that could be used by the government to try to change the division of labor between the sexes. This meant that each individual was gainfully employed.

The combination of Swedish labor market policy with family policy to support the drive for equality between women and men rests on forecasts of full employment in a long-term perspective. Some means of implementing general labor market policy such as the payment of moving allowances to persons/families who cannot get work in their home town; the provision of free manpower training with subsistence grants payable during the training period; and relief work and sheltered employment for displaced labor or the functionally unemployed. Thus, family policy in Sweden is trying to lighten the work burden of the two-income family to enable both parents to continue in their jobs while their children are growing up by providing them day-care facilities and other services for the families.[33]

But the dramatic increase was in the number of part-time jobs. From 1970 to 1980, 300,000 part-time workers joined the labor market. Nearly half of all working women have taken part-time jobs. (These are defined as less than 35 hours a week). Part-time work has increased, particularly among women with preschool children. The trend is more and more toward a larger part-time labor market for women with young children and a larger full-time labor market for men.

There is much to be said in favor of women working part-time. Child care is more easily arranged; children avoid having to spend long days at a day-care center, mothers have more time for their families and life is perhaps calmer and easier for everyone. At present, part-time workers have all the same social and vacation benefits as full-time workers. However, if more women work part-time it is because fewer women worked initially and part-time work protects children until good child care is available. This would have a great effect on equality. Equality and parenting to reinforce one another as themes requires that fathers should share parenting so that the mother's opportunities would not be limited.[34]

The egalitarian attitude of the Swedes forced them to provide the same services for foreign workers that they provide to their nationals. But since the price of that attitude is so costly, it prompted them to turn to their own untapped domestic supply of labor: women.

Conclusion

With the decrease in oil revenues of the Gulf states in the early 1980s, a foreign labor surplus was added to the problem facing the whole region. As a result, the Gulf states are now entering into a pause in their economic development. This pause is being used by the Gulf states to assess the economic and social problems brought about by rapid development and to develop a strategy that looks beyond the so-called 'oil glut'.[35]

Nevertheless, that 'pause' seems to be turning eventually into a crisis as the economy has passed through a more difficult phase in the last two years. Added to this problem was the crash of the unofficial stock market in Kuwait, which affected the Bahrain financial market and created a slow down of the economy similar to a recession. Needless to say, Bahrain and the other Gulf states were forced to reduce their spending and to make cutbacks in different essential projects.

In 1983, Bahrain's oil revenues dropped by $265 m. As a result, the 1982–85 four-year development plan was extended into 1987. Total investment under the plan is projected at around $5.8 b.[36]

A major consequence of the drop in oil production was the announcement of the Bahrain Petroleum Company (BAPCO) that it was reducing its work force by up to 25%. As a result, 1,000 workers were released. Of the company work force of 4,144, 17% are expatriates; plans are under way to reduce the expatriate work force by half whereas reduction of the Bahrain work force will be implemented gradually.[37]

In Bahrain and the other Gulf states, no policy has yet been announced by officials for dealing with the problem of unwanted foreign workers. But no one expects at present that Bahrain would deal with them the way Nigeria did. Foreign workers in Nigeria were deported and thrown outside the Nigerian borders when the economic crisis first appeared after the oil glut of 1983. One can expect at some point that some measures will be undertaken to deport more of the unskilled workers, especially those who work in the construction field because the infrastructure is virtually completed. Other measures might be undertaken such as the non-renewal of contracts, the reduction of salaries and the replacement of European and American experts by more Asian skilled workers to cut expenses. The skilled foreign laborers are even more needed in most jobs that require specialization, which most indigenous workers lack. In other words, Bahrain and the Gulf states will be more dependent on skilled foreign workers for future development projects and for the maintenance of current projects.

However, no matter what the consequences of the surplus of foreign workers will be, the governments of the Gulf states should be even more determined to integrate the more indigenous population into the labor force, and that certainly should include women.

It is to the benefit of Bahrain to reduce the reliance on foreign workers by encouraging the integration of women into the labor force. It makes economic sense to employ women instead of importing foreigners, especially the skilled ones, as statistics have indicated that most women who have joined the labor force have been professional, skilled females.

Joining the labor market presents women with a new sense of economic independence, which is vital to changing their traditional self-image and concept. In addition, their financial status will be improved and they will play a greater role in the development process that is taking place in Bahrain at present.

It is well known that income, education, occupation and attitudes toward the education and employment of women are interrelated with each other, and a favorable attitude in one area will certainly affect attitudes in other areas. Integrating more women into the development process is considered an essential step in nation building. What is meant by development is not material economic development only. It is rather a qualitative change in how people think and relate to their environment. It is investing in human resources and training people to run their own country. Increasing the number of female nationals in the labor force would help as a partial solution to labor market demands and would limit the foreign labor threat. At the same time, it would improve the situation of women in particular and the society as a whole in general.

Notes

1. J. S. Birks and C. A. Sinclair, *Arab Manpower*, London: Croom Helm, 1980, p. 24.
2. Ismael Serageldin, James A. Socknat, Stace Birks, Bob Li and Clive A. Sinclair, *Manpower and International Labor Migration in the Middle East and North Africa* (a World Bank publication), Oxford University Press, 1983, p. 4.
3. J. S. Birks and C. A. Sinclair, op cit., 1980, p. 24.

4. J. S. Birks and C. A. Sinclair, 'Economic and Social Implications of Current Development in the Arab Gulf: the Oriental Connection', in Niblock, Tim (Ed.], *Social and Economic Development in the Arab Gulf*, London: Croom Helm; New York: St Martin's Press, 1980, p. 138.
5. Ian J. Seccombe, 'Labor Migration to the Arabian Gulf: Evolution and Characteristics 1920–1950', *British Society for Middle Eastern Bulletin*, 10 (1): 3–10, 1983, p. 7.
6. *Ibid.*, p. 11.
7. *Ibid.*, p. 16.
8. J. S. Birks and C. A. Sinclair, *Arab Manpower*, London: Croom Helm, 1980, p. 168.
9. Nadir Fargani, 'The Problem of Foreign Labor in The Arab Gulf: The Extent of Composition of Manpower and Residents', *Al-Mustaqbal Al-Arabi*, vol. 4, no. 50, (April 1983), pp. 68–78 (Arabic).
10. Foad Khuri, *Tribe and State in Bahrain: The Transformation of Social and Political Authority in an Arab State*, Chicago and London: University of Chicago Press, 1980, p. 139.
11. Ismael Serageldin, James A. Socknat, Stace Birks, Bob Li and Clive A. Sinclair, *Manpower and International Labor Migration in the Middle East and North Africa* (a World Bank publication), Oxford University Press, 1983, p. 42.
12. *Ibid.*, p. 43.
13. *Ibid*, p. 41.
14. Nadia Youssef, 'Education and Female Modernism in Muslim World', *Journal of International Affairs*, vol. 30, no. 2 (1976–77), p. 202.
15. Ishaq Qutub, 'Urbanization in contemporary Arab Gulf States', *Ekistics*, vol. 50, no. 300 (May 1983) pp. 170–182.
16. Nadir Fargani, *Manpower Problems and Projections in the Gulf*, in El-Azhari, M. S. (Ed.), *The Impact of Oil Revenues on Arab Gulf Development*, Center for Arab Gulf Studies, University of Exeter. Croom Helm, London & Sidney, 1981, p. 164.
17. Baqir al-najjar, 'Thuruf'Amal wa Ma'ishat al-Ummal al-Ajanib Fi Aqtar al-khalij al-'Arabi', (The Living Condition of Foreign Labor in the Arab Gulf States), in Fargani, Nadir, (Ed.), *Foreign Labor Force in the Arab Gulf States*, Center for Arab Unity Studies, (Beirut), the Arab Institute for Planning (Kuwait), 1983, p. 88, (Arabic).
18. Saad Eddin Ibrahim, *The New Arab Social Order; A Study of the Social Impact of Oil Wealth*, Boulder, Col.: Westview Press; London: Croom Helm, 1982, p. 12.
19. Ismael Serageldin, James A. Socknat, Stace Birks, Bob Li and

Clive A. Sinclair, *Manpower and International Labor Migration in the Middle East and North Africa* (a World Bank publication), Oxford University Press, 1983, p. 50).
20. 'Bahrain: Identity Cards To Be Introduced', *Mideast Markets*, 11 (17): 2–3, (20 Aug. 1984) pp. 2–3.
21. 'Rising Racism on the Continent', *Time Magazine*, 6 Feb. 1984, p. 41.
22. 'Betrayed North Africans in France', *The Middle East Magazine*, Ashford, England, no. 120, Oct. 1984, p. 15.
23. 'Rising Racism in the Continent', *Time Magazine* 6 Feb. 1984, p. 41.
24. *Ibid.*, p. 45.
25. Philip Martin and Mark Miller, 'Guest Workers: Lessons from Europe', *Industrial and Labor Relations Review*, vol. 33, Apr. 1980 p. 321.
26. *Ibid.*, p. 319.
27. Rein Van Gendt, *Return to Migration and Reintegration Services*, Organization for European Cooperation & Development (OECD), Paris, 1977.
28. Karl Andersson, *With the Same Right as Others: About Migrants on the Swedish Labor Market* (the Swedish Institute), Sweden, 1979, p. 87.
29. Amika Baude, *Public Policy and Changing Family Patterns in Sweden, 1930–1977*, National Board of Health and Welfare, Stockholm, p. 150.
30. Gunnar Qvist, Joan Acker and Val R. Lorwin, 'Sweden', in Cook, Alice H., Lorin, Val R. and Daniels Arlene Kaplan (Eds), *Women and Trade Unions in Eleven Industrialized Countries*, Philadelphia: Temple University Press, 1984, p. 263.
31. *Ibid.*, p. 151.
32. Brigitta Wistrand, *Swedish Women on the Move*, (The Swedish Institute), Sweden, 1981, p. 50.
33. Rita Liljestrom, 'Sweden', in Kamerman, Sheila and Kahn, Alfred, (Eds), *Family Policy: Government and Families in Fourteen Countries*, Columbia University Press, 1978, pp. 19–48.
34. Sheila Kamerman and Alfred Kahn, *Child Care, Family Benefits, and Working Parents: A Study in Comparative Policy* New York: Columbia University Press, 1981, p. 235.
35. Francois M. Dickman, 'Economic Realities in the Gulf', *American Arab Affairs*, no. 7 winter 1983–84 Washington, D.C., p. 52.
36. 'Bahrain's Oil Revenues Estimated to Fall by 265 Million Dollars in 1983', *Middle East Economic Survey*, 26 (24), (28 March 1983).
37. 'Bahrain: BAPCO Plans to Cut Labor Costs', *Middle East Economic Digest*, 27 (34), 26 August 1983.

Chapter Two

Bahrain and the Gulf Cooperation Council (GCC)

> The affairs of Bahrain are reflections of the greater society, the Gulf and Arabia, to which the country belongs. It is difficult to believe that Bahrain, the little islands, could alone institute democracy while other states and principalities in the Gulf and Arabia continue to be ruled by tribally based governments.[1]

Bahrain: Background Notes

Bahrain is an archipelago of 33 islands of which only 5 are inhabited. It is located approximately half-way along the west coast of the Gulf between Saudi Arabia and Qatar. The total area of Bahrain is 663 sq. km. The main island is Bahrain, from which the country takes its name and where the capital, Manama, is located (see map of Bahrain Islands).

The total population of Bahrain was 350,798 in 1981 and is expected to increase to 470,786 in 1991.[2] However, the growth of the population over the last 40 years has increased four times, from 89,970 in 1941, when the census was first conducted, to 350,798 in 1981 (Table 2.1). During this period the Bahraini population increased 3.2 times and the non-Bahraini population 7 times.

The non-Bahraini population increased sharply from 37,889 in 1971 to 112,378 in 1981. This increase could be related to the expansion in the economy after the sharp increase of the price of oil in 1973. The growth in the foreign population rate caused many problems and created great resentment among nationals (see Chapter One).

The nationals, who form 68% of the total population,

Table 2.1 *Absolute and percentage distribution for population by nationality, sex ratio and census years (1941–81)*

Census years	Sex Ratio	Percentage M	F	T	Population Total
1941:					
Bahraini	—	—	—	82.29	74,040
Non-Bahraini	—	—	—	17.71	15,930
Total	—			100.00	89,970
1950:					
Bahraini	—	—	—	83.15	91,179
Non-Bahraini	—	—	—	16.85	18,471
Total	—	—	—	100.00	109,650
1959:					
Bahraini	101.9	50.46	49.54	82.95	118,734
Non-Bahraini	264.6	72.57	27.43	17.05	24,401
Total	118.5	54.23	45.77	100.00	143,135
1965:					
Bahraini	101.3	50.32	49.68	78.93	143,814
Non-Bahraini	237.5	70.37	29.63	21.07	38,389
Total	120.0	54.55	45.45	100.00	182,203
1971:					
Bahraini	101.5	50.38	49.62	82.47	178,193
Non-Bahraini	234.0	70.06	29.94	17.53	37,885
Total	116.6	53.83	46.17	100.00	216,078
1981:					
Bahraini	101.2	50.30	49.70	67.97	238,420
Non-Bahraini	308.5	75.52	24.48	32.03	112,378
Total	140.3	58.38	41.62	100.00	350,798

Sources: Statistical Abstracts 1983, op. cit., derived from Table 6, p. 16.

(238,420) are divided into two sects of Islam: Sunni and Shi'a. The size of the Shi'a population is not publicly known, but it is estimated to vary from 60–70% of the total nationals.[3] In addition, the Shi'a are generally regarded as the original inhabitants of Bahrain and constitute the poorer section of the population. The majority live in villages. Most of them are of Arab origin and few are of Persian origin. The Sunni, on the other hand, are sub-divided into Arab tribals: those who came originally from the Arabian peninsula, and those whose origin is the West Coast of Iran, the Huwala Arabs – who generally work as merchants and live in urban areas.[4]

In a field research in Bahrain, Khuri carried out a comprehensive household survey to measure the socio-economic variations and the discrepancies between social and ethnic groups that resulted from the development of oil. The survey covered 1,249 households. In the survey, the people of Bahrain were classified socially into seven categories:[5] the ruling family of Al-Khalifa, the Sunni of tribal origin, the urban Sunni, the urban Arab Shi'a, the Persian Shi'a, the rural Arab Shi'a and rural Shi'a living in suburban settlements. These seven categories were cross-compared in relation to education, income, occupation; and education and the employment of women. Some of his findings are summarized below:

1. About 70% of the income earners in Bahrain are salaried personnel. The Sunni of tribal origin, including the Al-Khalifa ruling family, have a complete monopoly on defense and security. The urban segment, Sunni or Shi'a, Arab or Persian, is concentrated in civil employment, professional careers (medical doctors and engineer), secretarial work or skilled labor. The Shi'a who live in villages or within suburban settlements predominate in unskilled salaried jobs. The rest (30%) of the income earners are merchants and traders who earn their living independently.
2. As for educational level, the urban group ranks higher in the upper educational levels than the other groups. The urban Sunni, poor or rich, permit the education and employment of women at a much higher rate than the tribal Sunni, whereas the rural Shi'a who live in suburban settlements are the least encouraging as far as the education of girls is concerned.
3. Income variation shows that the high income categories are dominated by the urban population and the lower categories by other populations. But the most striking features of his findings was that the high-income families (urban Sunni and Shi'a) permit the employment of unmarried sons and daughters at a much higher rate than the low income families. Low-income families (tribal Sunni and Shi'a who live in suburban settlements) generally have a very low rate of employment of unmarried sons or daughters.
4. Finally, one important finding was that achievement in

education and the employment of women is associated with other behavioral characteristics such as the composition and size of the household and the size of the family. These characteristics vary substantially by income and education, more so than by social origin. This means that people of high income or of high educational attainment share similar behavioral characteristics, regardless of their religious, ethnic or social categories.

POLITICAL DEVELOPMENT

Bahrain has been ruled by the Al-Khalifa family since 1782. The British began contacts with the Al-Khalifa as early as 1820, when a 'general treaty' was signed between Bahrain and the East India Company. Other peace and friendship treaties were signed with Great Britain in 1861, 1880 and 1892 respectively. These treaty arrangements strengthened the British rule in Bahrain and secured the Al-Khalifa rule over Bahrain. At the same time the treaties induced greater British involvement in the internal affairs of Bahrain. In 1919, after World War I, the British reconsidered their policy in Bahrain and moved beyond recommending reforms to the ruler. They intended to induce reforms through the civil courts, municipalities, schools and other modernizing institutions. Such reforms were opposed by many conservative groups, especially those of tribal origin. Those groups were led by the ruler's brother, who was considered as a symbol of tribal power.

In 1921, the British tried to eliminate tribal power by introducing administrative reforms. Such reforms became the major political issue in Bahrain, and then divided the people into two polarities: one composed of peasants and urban Shi'a, who suffered from the lack of standardized law and who favored the reforms, and the other of tribal groups and the merchants who opposed the reforms. The merchants feared the loss of privileges in trade, port facilities and custom duties. Many merchants paid very little tax on their imports. Tribal chiefs considered the reforms a threat to their sovereignty. However, by 1929 the reforms were fully set in operation.[6]

The administrative and bureaucratic reforms limited the power of tribal groups and of the urban merchant class. In addition, the reforms reorganized public services and economic resources, including pearl production, palm cultivation, fish traps, imports and exports. The new specialized public services focused on the court system, the state police and the various services and civil departments, which later became specialized ministries after independence in 1971.[7]

Political development was enhanced in the fifties when the Committee of National Union (CNU) was established in 1954. It consisted of 120 members representing different groups in Bahrain. During its 2 years of existence, the committee was able to fulfill several objectives: it obtained recognition from the government, negotiated with the British political agent as the country's sole popular organization, and forced the government of Bahrain to appoint a committee representing government, management and workers to prepare a draft of a labor ordinance. In 1956 the committee (CNU) was ordered by the government to break up and its leaders were tried and put in prison, and a state of emergency was declared.[8]

Britain's decision, in 1968 to withdraw from the Gulf by the end of 1971 created fear among the smaller Gulf states. In the same year, the British tried to establish a federation of Arab Emirates consisting of Bahrain, Qatar and the seven smaller shaikhdoms (Abud-Dhabi, Dubai, Sharjah, Ajman, Umm-al-Qawain, Ras-Alkhaimah and Fujairah).

The signing of the federation agreement was opposed by Iran because of its claim of sovereignty over Bahrain. Furthermore, Qatar and the seven Emirates had been suspicious that the federation might be dominated by Bahrain, whose population of 200,00 at that time outnumbered them all and whose economy was considered more developed than their own.[8] In addition, boarder disputes between Qatar and Bahrain over the Hawar Islands, which belong to Bahrain and were claimed by Qatar, were not solved. By 1970, Iran renounced its claims to Bahrain after the United Nations' special envoy's arrival in Bahrain in March–April 1970, at which time he recommended that Bahrain be granted independence. In August 1971, Bahrain proclaimed its independence. After independence, the Al-Khalifa tribal regime, based on the hereditary succession of rulers, was recognized as the legitimate form of government in Bahrain. The ruler exercises authority through a council of ministers, which since independence has been headed by the ruler's brother. Six ministers in the cabinet are also members of the Al-Khalifa family. They hold the most important ministries such as Defense, Interior, Foreign Affairs, Justice, Labor and Social Affairs, Housing and The Council for Youth and Sports. The remaining nine ministries are headed by commoners from both the Sunnah and Shi'a sects. They are appointed by the ruler of Bahrain. The other Gulf states have political systems similar to the system of Bahrain.

The United States' interest in Bahrain and the Gulf states became clearer in the last decade because of the increasing American concern with energy sources. Immediately after the British withdrawal from Bahrain and the Gulf region in 1971, the Bahrain government signed an agreement to lease to the US navy the formerly British-held Jufair naval Base.[10] The base is used to support the one navy flagship under the Middle East Force (MIDEASTFOR). The amount of rent the US was expected to pay Bahrain was $600,000 a year. Another agreement provided for an increase in the rent up to $4 m. However, the US and Bahrain reached a new agreement in June, 1977, that terminated the previous agreements of 1971 and 1975. The 1977 agreement stated that the US Middle East Force flagship could spend up to 120 days a year at the Jufair Base in Bahrain and that the rent would be reduced from $4 m to $2 m a year.[11]

LABOR DEVELOPMENT

An organized labor movement began to develop with the discovery of oil in the early 1930s. Since then, labor's determination to unionize has been a main cause for most of the political crises. The first labor strike in 1938 focused on two demands: a pay rise and better working conditions. As a result of that strike, the Bahrain Petroleum Company (BAPCO) began to employ more Indian and Iranian workers. Since these workers were not directly concerned with the country's political life, they would accept lower wages and be more loyal than Bahraini workers.[12]

The political development from 1954–56, when the Committee of the National Union was established, helped in the formation of the General Trade Union (GTU). The GTU was very popular among workers, who joined in great numbers. However, in 1956, the government crushed the union, jailed its leaders and banned all its activities; since then the union has been underground.

Another major strike started in 1965 at Bahrain Petroleum Company (BAPCO) and was supported by the majority of the people. The strike lasted for 3 months; then the strike was crushed by the government and the strikers were forced to go back to work.

The 1973 elections for the first National Assembly strengthened the labor movement significantly; it brought 30 elected members to the parliament. Three political groupings emerged. The Islamic group had six members; the leftists had eight members; and the rest of the members were in the center. In addition, there were fourteen cabinet members who acted as full members of the parliament. The leftist group first forced a number of concessions related mainly to labor actions. As a result, 36 strikes affecting major companies took place during the first 6 months of 1974. The strikes brought an enormous improvement in wages and working conditions, raising the minimum wage by one-third. Eventually, leaders of the strike were arrested in 1974. In 1981, the government formed a 'joint consultative committee' between management and labor in eight major companies. The first objective of the committee was to present an alternative to the underground trade unionism. The second was to create a better image of the government, especially in relation to the Arab Labor Organization and the International Confederation of Arab Trade Unions, which keeps challenging the legitimacy of Bahrain membership in those two organizations.[13] Elections were held among workers in 1983, but the degree of autonomy the committee is allowed is very limited.

CONSTITUTIONAL REFORMS

Unlike the successful administrative reforms of the 1920s, constitutional reforms which occurred 50 years later survived for less than 2 years. They were formally ended by the Emir of Bahrain, who issued a decree on 26 August 1975 dissolving the National Assembly, in order to contain the growing influence of the opposition and to restore the power of the ruling family.

On 16 December 1971, following independence, a law to form a National Assembly was announced by the Ruler of Bahrain. One year later, the constitutional assembly, which consisted of 22 elected and 8 appointed members, legislated the constitution of Bahrain. By 7 December 1973, a National Assembly, composed of 30 elected members and 14 appointed ministers, was established.

Three blocs emerged in the National Assembly: the People's Bloc, the Religious Bloc and the Independent Middle. The People's Bloc included Communists, Socialists and Arab nationalists. The Bloc cut across sects and stood mostly for the rights of labor to unionize. The religious Bloc, at the other extreme, announced its opposition to such issues of Islamic concern as the sale of liquor, the policy of coeducation in higher education and the participation of females in public life. This Bloc had the backing of the rural Shi'a.[14] The Independent Middle, which varied in political commitments and in ideologies, has been able to work as a united bloc; this group has given support to both sides.

The 1973 election brought with it a stronger opposition to the government and more demands by labor activists. This situation made the government look vulnerable, weak and more defensive. To confront such a threat, the Emir of Bahrain issued a new law in December 1974, granting the government the right to arrest and imprison for 3 years, without trial, any person suspected of disturbing national security. The elected members of the National Assembly did not approve of implementing the law. Consequently, in August 1975, when the government and the parliament members failed to reach an agreement on this matter, the Emir of Bahrain issued a decree dissolving the National Assembly. Some cannot dismiss the Saudi role in dissolving the parliament and claim that Saudi Arabia was putting pressure on the Emir 'to suspend his experiment in representative government and to dismiss the National Assembly on the grounds that they were a source of danger to the area's stability'.[15] With the dissolving of the National Assembly, the democratization of the tribal regime proved to be a failed experiment.

ECONOMIC DEVELOPMENT

Prior to the discovery of oil in the early 1930s, the Bahrain economy depended upon three major sources of revenues: pearl diving, agriculture and trade. Other sources such as fishing and boat building were of less importance. This meant that the sea, which supported pearl-diving, fishing and trade activities, was the main source of economic activity.[16]

The pearl industry flourished in the 1920s, when the size of the Bahraini pearl diving fleet was established and consisted of 500 ships. In the 1930s, the pearl diving industry witnessed a rapid decline because of the international monetary crisis and the growth of the cultured pearl industry in Japan. By 1950 the pearl industry declined to the extent that there was not a single diver employed in the industry.[17]

As for agriculture, the cultivated area of Bahrain is very small and is estimated to cover 10% of the total area of Bahrain. The main agricultural products were and still are dates and alfalfa. The decline of agriculture had started in the 1920s and continued until the 1960s. Many social and economic factors contributed to such decline; the system of land tenure was the main social factor whereas dwindling water resources and the scarcity of crop marketing were the major economic factors.[18] Other factors are related to the economic order that emerged with the oil industry, which made palm cultivation a luxury investment. The demand for dates decreased as a result of the changing dietary habits of the Bahraini population; also, the collapse of the pearl fishing industry added to such decline because a large part of the dates produced had been eaten by pearl divers at sea.[19] A new agricultural development is hydroponic and greenhouse agriculture, which has been developed since 1981. At present, Bahrain produces 65% of the eggs it consumes and 35% of its poultry.

Trade could be considered to be the only sector that continued to flourish between Bahrain, the Gulf ports and the Eastern coast of Africa and India. The growth of foreign trade made more Bahrainis turn to investment in this sector. With the expansion of port facilities in 1953 and the establishing of a Free Trade Zone in 1957, the re-export trade began to flourish and many agencies for import–export were set up in Bahrain. All the Gulf states, especially Saudi Arabia, were customers of Bahrain's re-export trade. The situation changed in the 1960s, and trade started declining when the Gulf states established their own port facilities and started importing directly from different places.

Industry, on the other hand, faced a difficult time from the beginning. The discovery of oil in 1932, made the traditional industries and agriculture (palm cultivation, textiles and pottery) lose their market value, and only a few were kept through government subsidies. At the same time the Bahrain government made an attempt to encourage the diversification of industry. Such a policy helped Bahrain to cope with the recent regional recession better than any other Gulf state. The development of industry in such fields as oil and gas production, manufacturing industries, banking and finance, and tourism will be discussed in more detail:

Oil and gas production

Bahrain depends on oil for 60% of its revenue. In 1979, the government acquired full ownership of production resources. By 1982, the state-owned Bahrain National Company (BANACO) took over full responsibility for management of the onshore producing fields.

Other developments occured in oil refining when the Bahrain Petroleum Company (BAPCO) was restructured in 1981 as a 40–60 joint venture between the Caltex Petroleum Corporation and the Bahrain government to operate the 250,000 b/d refinery and the marine terminal.[20] The Bahrain National Gas Company (BANAGAS), for gas liquefaction, proved to be a successful investment because the associated gas that it uses as raw material had no previous economic value and was vented at the well heads.

Manufacturing industries

The first step towards industrial diversification was the establishing of Aluminium Bahrain (ALBA) in 1971. The plant was at first unsuccessful, but later it was modernized and increased production while at the same time reducing its work force from nearly 3,000 to 1,800.[21]

The Arab Shipbuilding and Repair Yard (ASRY) was funded and built by the Organization of Arab Petroleum Exporting Countries (OAPIC) in 1977. At present, it employs 1,000 people. ASRY has effectively broadened its industrial base, introduced new technology and enhanced Bahrain's reputation as a maritime service center.[22]

Other industrial projects have been constructed in the last few years and financed mostly by Arab and Gulf states; such projects as the Arab Iron and Steel Company (AISCO), at a cost of $300 m, and the Gulf Petrochemical Industries Company

(GPIC), have added to the diversification of modern industry in Bahrain.

Small-scale industry has been encouraged by the government recently, with incentives given to the private sector to start small industrial projects. Such incentives include the provision of feasibility studies, concessionary land leases in industrial areas and a 'free zone' for exports.

Banking and finance

In recent years, Bahrain has become an international financial center. It has the advantage of having a time-zone midway between Europe and the Far East and good telecommunications and air link.

The Bahrain offshore banking market was estimated at $62 b in 1985. The number of Offshore Banking Units (OBUs) in Bahrain is nearly 100; there are also more than 12 specially licensed investment banks and 61 foreign bank representative offices. Such expansion required a more sophisticated, well-trained labor force. To meet such requirements, a unit for training in banking and finance was established in 1983.

The situation of OBUs in Bahrain started deteriorating in 1985. A few banks have started pulling out from Bahrain; 17 OBUs have decided to close their operations recently, and more are planning to pull out in the near future. Many factors could have attributed to such deterioration; the decrease in oil revenue in the Gulf region, poor international banking conditions and changes in Saudi monitary policy. Saudi Arabia, the main customer for OBUs, has imposed protectionism since 1983. As a result, many smaller offshore banks began moving towards new directions, mainly investment banking.

Tourism

Tourism is more recent in Bahrain. The government is paying more attention to this sector as part of its policy of economic diversification. Tourism in general has a great impact on society. It requires economic, social and even architectural adjustments. It also requires importing foreign labor to work in occupations in which nationals do not work. In general, the impact of tourism on local societies is very great.

Table 2.2 *Hotels, rooms and beds by grade (1977–84)*

	Year							
Grade	1977	1978	1979	1980	1981	1982	1983	1984
5 star hotels								
Hotels	4	5	5	7	9	9	9	9
Rooms	791	1,092	1,092	1,716	2,298	2,298	2,298	2,298
Beds	1,170	1,917	1,917	2,848	3,768	3,768	3,868	3,868
4 star hotels								
Hotels	7	11	11	13	13	13	13	14
Rooms	454	721	721	846	846	846	766	887
Beds	837	1,389	1,383	1,651	1,651	1,651	1,631	2,019
3 star hotels								
Hotels	5	4	3	4	5	5	5	5
Rooms	197	112	79	112	128	128	128	128
Beds	365	210	158	210	242	242	242	242
Total								
Hotels	16	20	19	24	27	27	27	28
Rooms	1,442	1,925	1,892	2,674	3,274	3,272	3,193	3,313
Beds	2,372	3,516	3,458	4,709	5,661	5,661	5,741	6,129

Sources: Statistical Abracts 1984, op. cit., derived from Table 14.05, p. 355

Tourists come to Bahrain mostly from the Gulf regions. In 1979, the total number of tourists reached 129,016, nearly 74% of them came from the Gulf states. In 1983, the number of tourists increased to reach 182,781. Nearly 84% of them came from the Gulf states. Because of the increase of tourists, new hotels were built. In 977, there were 16 hotels in Bahrain. By 1984, the number increased to 28 hotels with 3,193 rooms and 6,129 beds (See Table 2.2).

In addition, the government and the private sector are planning a tourist attraction center (an Arabian style Disneyland) in the Zallaq area. This project will cost $180 m and will include a luxury hotel complex on a man-made island, beach villas, chalets, condominiums and a marina.

The Department of Tourism supervises all hotels, travel agencies and tourist activities, including guides, gift shops and restaurants. Training programs for department employees have been arranged in Bahrain and abroad.

Many factors have contributed to the flourishing of this new sector:

1. Bahrain is situated in the center of the Gulf; it takes only a few minutes to get there by plane: 10 minutes from Saudi Arabia, 45 minutes from Kuwait and 30 minutes from Qatar. Furthermore, the completion of the causeway that links Bahrain to Saudi Arabia and the rest of the Gulf states is expected to play an important role in enhancing tourism and will make it more convenient for tourists to come by car.
2. Bahrain is the only Gulf state that permits the sale of alcohol and drinking in public places such as hotels and restaurants. This encourages many foreigners who work all over the Gulf to spend their weekends in Bahrain.
3. Bahrain is famous for its beautiful beaches, marina clubs, horse races, excellent hotels, night clubs and public parks.
4. Historically, Bahrain is considered the center of folklore, dances and songs in the Gulf region. Tourists from the Gulf are attracted to such entertainment.

Politically and economically, Bahrain sees its future in the Gulf Cooperation Council (GCC). In the following paragraphs, the GCC formation and its impact on Bahrain will be discussed in more detail.

The Gulf Cooperation Council

The establishment of the Gulf Cooperation Council in May 1981 was an attempt to pool resources to safeguard the 'stability' of the region and to improve cooperation in politics, economics and security matters. A kind of loose political confederation is under consideration by all members of six Gulf states, which include Saudi Arabia, Kuwait, Bahrain, Oman, Qatar and the United Arab Emirates. (See map of the Gulf Cooperation Council states). The population of the Gulf Cooperation Council (GCC) was estimated in 1980–81 to exceed 13 million (Table 2.3). The six states cover an area of 2,557,277 sq.km. and contribute nearly half of the OPEC oil production. In addition, the GCC contains 40% of the world's oil reserves.

The GCC began implementing several important measures to reduce barriers to the movement of capital, labor and products among its member states. Citizens among the GCC member

Table 2.3 *Population and military power in the GCC states*

State	Population	Size of Armed Forces	Military Participation Ratio*
Saudi Arabia	8–12,000000†	51,500	0.004
Kuwait	1,450,000	12,400	0.009
Bahrain	400,000	2,700	0.007
Qatar	260,000	6,000	0.023
UAE	1,130,000	49,000	0.043
Oman	970,000	23,550	0.024

Sources: Orbis, Autumn 1984, op. cit., derived from Table 2, p. 495.

† Military balance figures for Saudi's population tend to be high; a more common figure is 5,000,000, giving a participation ratio of .01.

* The military participation ratio is calculated by dividing size of armed force by population.

states can now work and invest freely in business within the GCC area. The six member states started out by seeking agreement on the least controversial issues. For example, telephone charges have been standardized throughout member states, and power and water charges will follow. In 1983, a GCC Unified Economic Agreement was reached among the six states setting the stage for interstate business regulations, free movement of vehicles, unified custom levies, labor regulations, foreign ownerhsip regulations and similar issues. In the future, unified passports will be issued to the nationals of the six states.

Since its formation in 1981, the GCC has been equated with the preservation of Gulf security and stability. Although committees have been established to coordinate social, economic, cultural and informational activities among the member states, most of the activities of the GCC have focused on security and, to a lesser extent, on economic matters. The member states of the GCC share traditional family regimes, based on tribal affiliations, which had been strengthened under British colonial rule. The six states have no history of sustained decolonization struggles, and nearly 5 million of its population of 13 million are immigrant workers.[23]

Security problems are the main source of threat; both external as well as internal threats are destabilizing the Gulf regimes. The outbreak of the war between Iraq and Iran in 1980 prompted the Gulf states to establish the GCC; they feared a possible spread of war over the whole region. Although the GCC has been most successful in resolving local disputes and working for economic integration, it has failed to help in ending the Gulf war. Another external source of threat for the Gulf states is the reliance on the shipping of their oil through the strategic Straits of Hormuz, a situation that became of a great concern; the Iranian threat to block Gulf tankers is causing deep fears.[24] However, the GCC states are thinking of ways to resolve such problems; plans are underway to build a crude oil pipeline linking Gulf oil fields with an export terminal in the Indian Ocean. Another pipeline would run from Kuwait along the Gulf coast through Saudi Arabia and the United Arab Emirates to Fujairah, in the Indian Ocean. A study will be conducted in Saudi Arabia for feasibility and cost.[25]

Internal problems as well are confronting GCC regimes because of the rapid social changes induced by the enormous growth of their economies. New social classes have developed rapidly, among them is a growing educated middle class. Foreign laborers outnumber nationals; statistics in 1981 show that foreigners constitute a high percentage of the Gulf population. In Kuwait, for example, the percentage of foreigners constitute 73%, whereas in Qatar they form 60%. Only in Oman do they form a mere 22% of the population although here too their number is growing rapidly.

The GCC states share fundamental similarities and have a better chance for integration than any other group:

1. They share traditional family regimes, based on tribal affiliations. Such similarities in regimes and in state structures have been the main reason for the successful cooperation and coordination of internal security policies by GCC member states.[26]
2. All the GCC states lack an industrial infrastructure, indigenous manpower and technical expertise.
3. They all depend on large numbers of migrant workers from different nationalities and on western technical expertise.
4. They all depend upon oil as a single resource in developing their economy.
5. They all depend on a large foreign personnel as far as

security is concerned; these are recruited mainly from Pakistan.

In all the six states, the tribal political system is headed by a ruler who retains absolute power. Political participation does not exist in any Gulf state. Saudi Arabia and Oman have no written constitutions. In Saudi Arabia, the ultimate law is derived from the Quran and the sovereignty resides in the King, whereas in Oman the Sultan is the absolute ruler. In the UAE and Qatar, the National Assembly members are appointed by the ruler; no elections have ever been held in either state.[27] Only in Kuwait and Bahrain, where constitutions were proclaimed in 1962 and 1973 respectively, have National Assemblies been popularly elected by males over 21 years of age. However, in 1975, the National Assembly in Bahrain was dissolved by the Emir of Bahrain; then, Kuwait followed suit and dissolved its National Assembly ending 14 years of 'democratic' rule. Later, in 1981, Kuwait resumed elections until July 1986, when the National Assembly was dissolved and several articles of the constitution were suspended by the Emir of Kuwait. This failure of the democratic experiment in Kuwait and Bahrain and the failure of other Gulf states to even attempt democratic rule proved that the strength of tribal rule eliminates any chance for a participatory government.[28]

SECURITY OF THE GCC

The United States, Western Europe and Japan have a growing interest in the Gulf region. For the United States, the GCC ranks after Europe as the vital area of economic and strategic concern.[29] The US imports nearly 5% of its energy from the Gulf, but its allies, Japan and Western Europe, depend for their energy on Gulf oil. In addition, the US is trying to deter the USSR from seizing the Gulf oil fields.

The United States has supported the creation of the GCC to provide a force to be used when the need arises. The US rationale is that the GCC is responsible for the internal security functions. This, as well as the bilateral security agreements for joint intervention among the GCC states, should minimize the need for direct US intervention in the event of internal upheaval.[30]

The GCC is already seeking to improve its military power (Table 2.3). However, it cannot overcome many factors beyond its capacity – such factors including the small size of its population, its limited industrial base and its lack of available manpower to prevent any major military build-up.[31]

In order to overcome the military personnel shortage, the GCC states hired thousands of foreign workers to work in the defense sectors. Military officers from different states serve on contract in the Gulf region, with Pakistanis dominating in every nation. Moreover, it seems that the more Gulf states modernize their forces, the more they are dependent on foreign personnel who understand the sophisticated weapons. Government control over the military is enhanced by foreign personnel, because it is believed that their loyalty is to their pay masters; national personnel who work in the military cannot be trusted because 'it is difficult to find nationals who are both loyal to the regime and technically efficient'.[32]

PROJECTS IN BAHRAIN FINANCED BY THE GCC STATES

Politically and economically, Bahrain associates its future with the GCC. With the impending depletion of oil resources in the early 1990s, Bahrain has had to look for other income resources; in other words, it has had to diversify its industry and business. Other rich Gulf states, especially Saudi Arabia, helped Bahrain with its decision on a diversification of income resources. The Gulf states chose Bahrain as the site for a number of industrial projects.

At present, there are many projects in Bahrain, constructed and financed by the GCC states. With the economic agreement signed in 1983 among the six Gulf states, Bahrain, in particular, gained a wider market for the sale of its industrial products. This agreement called for the elimination of tariffs between member states, and the immediate consequence of the agreement was an increase in trade between the six Gulf states. This new industry added to the revenue. At the same time, a large number of women had the opportunity to be employed in the new industry, mostly in clerical jobs but some in the middle management level. Projects that were financed by the GCC states will be discussed in the following paragraphs.

The ammonia and methanol complex of the Gulf Petrochemical Industries Company (GPIC) was built in 1985 by Kuwait, Bahrain and Saudi Arabia. The company is 40% owned by Bahrain and 60% by Kuwait and Saudi Arabia. Another large project was built in 1984 by the Arab Iron and Steel Company (AISCO) Pelletising, which cost $300 m.

Bahrain was picked as a center for the joint venture Gulf and Arab industries even before the formation of the GCC. For example, the Arab Shipbuilding and Repair Yard (ASRY) was built and funded by the Arab Petroleum Exporting Countries (OAPIC). At present, ASRY employs 1,000 people, of whom Bahraini females constitute a larger number. Furthermore, ASRY has effectively broadened the industrial base, introduced new technology and enhanced Bahrain's reputation as a maritime service center.[33] Aluminium Bahrain (ALBA) Smelter, which is based on natural gas, was built in 1971. In 1979 the Saudi government became a 20% shareholder in ALBA, after having helped to finance the company because it ran into problems with unsold metal. The company is achieving some gains at present; it has reduced its work force from about 3,000 in 1976/77 to 1,800, while still increasing production every year. Financial projects also found a fertile ground in Bahrain; the creation in 1980 of the Arab Insurance Group (ARIG) made Bahrain an important insurance center in the Middle East. The company is owned by Kuwait, Lybia and the United Arab Emirates.

Educational cooperation has been strengthened by the establishment of the Arabian Gulf University (AGU) in 1983. This project could be considered to be a model of scientific cooperation among the Gulf states. Iraq also is a partner, along with the six Gulf states, in financing and setting the policy of the University. Programs in oceanography, and in the science of deserts and arid lands, are designed in relation to the region's environment. Unlike Bahrain University, the Gulf University is not coeducational. The university plans, within the coming 20 years, to reach the goal of serving some 5,000 students. In its primary stage, the main campus in Sakhir will be able to enroll 2,000 students, in addition to those of the College of Medicine and Medical Science, which admitted its fourth class of students in 1985/86. The College of Education will be opened in 1986/87.

Finally, the Saudi–Bahrain causeway is the most important project that will affect Bahrain's future for a long time. The twenty-mile causeway that cost $1 bn takes 20 mintues to cross and is able to carry 2,700 vehicles an hour. With the completion of the causeway in December 1985, Saudi military access to the political influence in Bahrain will be even greater.[34] The causeway may have some military uses.

Many have an ambivalent feeling about the causeway. They fear that the society made more accessible by the causeway has to introduce some restrictions similar to those that apply on the mainland, especially restrictions on the rules governing the women in Saudi Arabia. Others admit that the causeway 'is good for business but not for Bahrainis'.[35] However, in the first 3 months since its official opening, the causeway proved to be a blessing for the majority of the Bahrainis, especially those with limited income who suffer from the overpriced goods and food items. Thousands of people cross the causeway every day to buy the heavily subsidized food products and goods from Saudi Arabia. As a result, the average spending of a middle-income family has been reduced by half. Such families are thought to be saving nearly $250–300 each month. For better or worse, Bahrain will be physically integrated to the mainland of Arabia; there will be more Bahrainis seeking jobs in the wider Saudi job market, and at the same time, many Saudi families will settle in Bahrain, especially those who seek modern education for their children and a more relaxing social atmosphere for their families.

The Present Situation of Women in the Gulf States

Women's situation in the Gulf states is similar to that of Arab and Moslem women in the Middle East. This means they are deprived of many privileges granted to their male counterparts. Family law remains a key issue for women in the Gulf region. All the Gulf states except Kuwait still practice the 1,500-year-old 'Shari'a' code: a rigid Islamic law that ensures segregation of the sexes and discriminates against women in matters such as inheritance, divorce, child custody and in other issues regarding family. Even the Kuwaiti family law, which was issued in 1984, does not offer many rights for Kuwaiti women.

As for employment, women in the Gulf states constitute a low percentage of the work force; in Kuwait, working women formed 10% of the work force in 1980, in Qatar they formed nearly 4.2% in 1981, and in Bahrain they formed 8.3% of the total labor force. Women in general have made the most progress in the public sector, where they work in teaching, nursing and in clerical jobs; a few work as doctors, technicians and police officers. However, there is a growing realization among manpower planners in the Gulf states that women could play a significant part in the economy, thus reducing the need to bring in so much immigrant labor.

Women's condition in the Gulf states differs to a certain extent from one state to the other because the degree of advancement in overall development is not the same in each of the Gulf states. In education, for example, Bahrain was the pioneer among all Gulf states; it started public education for both sexes at the beginning of this century whereas the UAE and Oman only started such programs in the 1950s and 1970s respectively.

In the following pages, each state will be discussed in more detail. (Bahraini women will be discussed in Chapter Three.)

KUWAIT

Kuwaiti women are thought to be moving towards modernization at a greater speed than any other women in the Gulf states and are even enjoying wages similar to those of men. In the labor force, Kuwaiti women's participation increased significantly from 3% in 1970 to 10% in 1980.[36] Furthermore, a number of Kuwaiti females are holding such high positions as under-secretary assistants in the ministries of education and social affairs and labor. Other Kuwaiti women have become deans at Kuwait University.

Many factors account for the relatively rapid development of Kuwaiti women. Kuwait per capita income reached $19,850 in 1982, which is considered the highest in the world. In addition, Kuwait started its phase of social and economic development and gained independence in 1961, earlier than any other Gulf state. With the establishment of Kuwait University in 1965 the pace of development was accelerated, and a great number of females, who did not have the chance to go abroad for higher education, were able to pursue their education in Kuwait. In the past decade, 64% of Kuwait University graduates were females.[37]

With the access to education (which brought with it greater job opportunity), the number of Kuwaiti women in the labor force increased. In 1970 only 2% of the total Kuwaiti women were in the labor force, whereas in 1980 the number increased to 10%.

Women's organizations in Kuwait took the lead among the Gulf women and held regional conferences in 1975, 1981, 1984 and 1986: the Women's Cultural Society, headed by Lulwa Al-Qatami, took the initiative in organizing women's efforts in the region. Most representatives of women's organizations from the Gulf states attended the conferences. Many issues concerning women were discussed – such issues as the role of women in economic and social development and, in particular, the role of women in the labor force. There were other issues such as education, illiteracy among women, marriage, divorce and the need to have family law replace the out-dated Shari'a law. This resulted in the formation of a committee, based in Kuwait, for coordination and cooperation among women in the Gulf region.

Kuwaiti women also led the way for political advancement. After the elections in 1984, some liberal members in the Kuwaiti parliament brought forward a bill to grant women the vote. The parliament's legal committee consulted with the Ministry of Islamic Affairs, which issued a ruling that 'the nature of the electoral process befits men, who are endowed with ability and expertise; it is not permissible that women recommend or nominate other women or men'.[38] Some Kuwaitis saw the ruling as reflecting government opposition to female suffrage. Although the attempt to gain the right to vote was unsuccessful in general, it is a sign that shows that Kuwaiti citizens, including women, enjoy relative freedom denied to other Gulf citizens.

SAUDI ARABIA

Women in Saudi Arabia might be considered the most deprived compared to other women in the GCC states. Saudi Arabia implements the very strict Shari'a laws on issues regarding women and family. Moreover, it is the only Gulf state where women are not allowed to drive cars; this makes them totally dependent on a male relative, either a husband, a close relative or a hired driver, to take them anywhere they need to go.

In keeping with the strict segregation of Saudi society, females are employed to run women's schools as teachers and as administrators. There are more than 20,000 women employed by the government in jobs where they work in different careers as teachers, physical therapists, social workers, administrators and doctors. This segregation gives women a professional advantage because there is no competition with men for such jobs.[39]

A working woman lives in two separate worlds in Saudi Arabia. As an active career woman, she contributes to society, but as a protected female, she is veiled in public and cannot leave her country for any reason without a relative as a guardian, a 'Mihrim'. This especially limits Saudi women who are not allowed to attend conferences or seminars or even to represent their government abroad even on an individual basis. With such severe restrictions facing employed women, few of them stay in their jobs – especially married women with children. In 1983, 30% of Saudi Arabia's 25,000 women teachers resigned, citing their husband's objections, the pressure of household responsibilities, poor transportation and the scarcity of nursery schools and day-care services as reasons.[40] However, there is still much debate in Saudi society on old and modern values concerning women and their role in development.

THE UNITED ARAB EMIRATES

Traditional Islamic and tribal values are dominant in UAE society. In recent years, some changes in marriage has been taking place in society, but Shari'a law remains the legal system governing all aspects of life.

Education has played a significant part in changing the role of women in the UAE. Prior to 1953, education was traditional, primarily religious, and was known all over the Gulf states as the 'Mutawwa'. Boys and girls spent unlimited time memorizing and reciting the Holy Qur'an. They 'graduated' whenever they finished the task of memorizing the Holy Book.

The first school was founded in 1953 and was limited to boys only. In 1964–65 two schools were founded for females. By 1971, females were encouraged by the government to pursue their higher education abroad. In addition, several social centers have been established in different locations to train women in such skills as cooking and home hygiene. The Women's Federation, which consists of all women's organizations and is headed by the Emir's wife, does similar work, in addition to raising money for charity and running kindergartens and literacy classes for illiterate females.

The spread of education among women has decreased the high

rate of illiteracy. In 1968, the illiteracy rate among women was as high as 91.1%; in 1975, it dropped to 61.1%. Educational opportunity for females increased when the University of Al-Ain was opened in 1977. This helped females achieve higher education.

Professionally, women in the UAE are largely working as social workers, teachers, or in the so-called 'feminine' occupations. However, as the educational level continues to rise, the situation of women in the UAE will be improved.[41]

QATAR

Women's development in Qatar started with the establishment of the first formal girl's school in 1955, 5 years after the discovery of oil. The education of women has been met with great opposition from men. One main objection to the education of women in Qatar was the fear that through education, women would learn how to write. Conservative men in Qatar thought that women should be taught only reading but not writing. (Reading meant mainly to be able to read the Holy Quran.) Men feared that the ability to write would enable women to communicate with men, an idea regarded as an immoral act in that conservative society.[42]

As a result of such opposition, the growth of education for women was very slow at the beginning. This was changed in recent years when the number of female students increased from 55 in 1955 to 19,356 in 1980/81.

The University of Qatar was established in 1973 and offered two faculties of education, one for men and one for women. There were 157 students, of whom 103 were women. At present, the number of female students studying at the university has reached 2,285, compared to 1530 male students.[43] This trend of a higher proportion of females in universities all over the Gulf region is mainly related to the fact that boys are sent abroad for higher education, whereas females are encouraged to join universities in their own countries, so they will not be exposed to new ideas and new challenges. However, most females who graduate from the university work as teachers; nearly half of the females in the work force (1,317 out of a total of 2,233) are employed in education.

The Qatari society is more conservative and more tribal than the societies of the rest of the Gulf states. Women are not allowed to drive cars; this privilege is limited only to a few working women. Furthermore, women are not allowed to form women's societies. It is only recently that they were granted permission to establish a branch of the Red Crescent Society. The Women's Branch of the Qatar Red Crescent Society, which was established in 1982, is the only women's association in Qatar.

OMAN

Human resources in Oman, like those in the rest of the Gulf region, are very limited. The majority of its one million population depend for their existence on agriculture and fishing.

Oman started the pace of development 16 years ago, after the discovery of oil. In 1970, Oman had only 3 schools, 30 teachers and 909 male students; by 1984 there were 561 schools, 9236 teachers and 195,400 students (116,692 male and 78,708 female).

Female employment increased very rapidly, especially in the government sector where it reached 2,510 or 8% of the total government employees in 1983. Furthermore, Omani women are holding different jobs, even jobs as pilots; many are recruited into the police force and some are even holding high administrative positions as directors and under secretaries.

In 1970, 'The Omani Women's Association' was established. By 1984, the Association had opened branches in five provinces, and 1132 members had joined from all over the country. The Omani Woman Association is participating in many different activities and programs concerning women, including eradicating illiteracy among women, organizing lectures and cultural activities, and taking part in international and regional conferences.

The Impact of the GCC Formation on Women's Development in Bahrain

Bahrain society has always been more cosmopolitan, pluralistic and less tribal than the societies of the other Gulf states. With the formation of the GCC in 1981, Bahrain became more integrated with the mainland of the Arabian Peninsula. The new situation could be described as a mixed blessing for women's advancement. Many projects worth billions of dollars were built and financed by the GCC states, especially Saudi Arabia. For such huge economic gains, Bahrain had to pay the price of becoming more conservative, and it has already started to slow down the pace of its social and political development.

Political development, which began after independence in 1971 with constitutional reforms and the elections of the first National Assembly in 1973, ended in failure when the National Assembly was dissolved in 1975. Social development also faced a growing conservative attitude from different conservative groups, especially from Islamic fundamentalist groups. These groups pressed the government to make concessions in civil laws and to force people to return to Shari'a law and to the basic teachings of Islam. Fundamentalist groups have also brought their efforts to bear on similar groups in GCC countries.

At the same time, women's organizations from all over the Gulf states were getting together and coordinating their efforts in order to gain more rights or even to resist what the Islamic and other conservative groups were trying to impose on them.

In general one can find some positive trends in women's employment, education and other aspects of development:

1. The formation of the GCC brought with it an improvement in the economy; some industrial projects have helped in strengthening and diversifying the economy of Bahrain. Such projects have increased the employment of men and women.
2. Tourism has been expanding in recent years with more tourists coming from the GCC states. More jobs were created in this sector, which was dominated by females.
3. The establishment of the Gulf University in Bahrain (with its various fields of specialization including marine science and medicine) has created a great opportunity for both sexes. Females who were not able to pursue their education abroad can now join the Gulf University. In addition, the Gulf University sent hundreds of nationals from Bahrain and the GCC abroad in order to be qualified for teaching at the university.

There are also some negative trends regarding women, which are described below:

1. The cooperation among the Gulf states has resulted in a

more conservative policy towards women; this is manifested in the segregation of the two sexes at the Gulf University.

2. There have been restrictions on the appointment of women to administrative positions in the public and private sectors. Some explain these restrictions as the conservative influence from GCC states.
3. Recently, the Ministry of Education in Bahrain changed its policy of sending academic achievers abroad regardless of their sexes. It is now reserving scholarships mostly for male students even though females often have the highest grades.
4. There has been a setback in the efforts of women's groups and other liberal groups to push the government to issue a modern family law. In specifying the effect of the formation of the GCC on women's advancement, one should not forget the most important overall gain – that Bahrain has become, once and forever, an integral part of the larger mainland of Arabia.

The Future of the Gulf Cooperation Council

Economic integration among the Gulf states was an important step towards strengthening political integration; people, goods, money and services can move freely as within a single country. Moreover, more integration means a larger market for long-term benefits, especially after the completion of the causeway. But there have been short-term disadvantages that have made many businessmen complain; for example, businessmen in Bahrain fear the competition of powerful businesses in the rich Gulf states, who are able to sell products at cheaper prices. Also, economic development in the region has created more diversification in the economy, but the economy might become more dependent than ever on the international oil market.

With the current decrease in oil revenues, the Gulf states are facing economic uncertainties they were not prepared to face in the last decade. The price of oil increased from $2.9 per barrel in 1973 to $13 in 1978 and kept increasing until it reached $34 in 1981. Some experts predictd that the price would rise even higher between 1980 and 1985, reaching $44 to $78 per barrel by the end of 1985. However, such predictions proved to be false. The GCC oil revenue dropped by half, from $145 billion to $72 billion.[44] Many factors contributed to this: the improvement in energy efficiency in the industrial countries, the growth of oil production in non-OPIC countries such as England and Norway, and the substitution in the industrial countries of other sources of energy for oil, including solar and atomic energy.

The impact of the loss of oil revenues is already being felt all over the Gulf region. All of the six states have started implementing a policy that calls for tightening expenditures. The consequences of the decreases in oil revenues could be stated as follows:

(a) A large number of industrial projects have been cancelled; the volume of workers in major services has been greatly reduced. In the private sector, the hiring of new employees has been restricted, and there has been no raise in salaries.

(b) In addition, people's expectations of a steady increase in their standard of living is creating a problem for the governments of the Gulf states, which have already started making some cuts in expenditure in medical, educational and other social services. In addition, the heavily subsidized water and electricity services will be forced to charge more.[45] As a matter of fact, Bahrain was the first of the Gulf states to increase charges on water and electricity consumption. This outraged many people, and the government is considering dropping the increase.

(c) Living standards have been maintained by large subsidies in all the Gulf states. With the decrease in oil revenues, the governments of the region might be forced to increase the charges for some of the vital services. The consequences will be the lowering of people's expectations.

(d) Another consequence of the decrease in oil revenues is the expected increase in bureaucratic inefficiency and corruption in the public sector. These are already becoming more serious.

(e) Women's programs might be affected as well. Social centers that offer women different kinds of training in sewing, literacy programs and handicrafts might lose a large amount of government funding.

(f) An expected widening of the gap between the rich and poor might worsen the social conflict among the two classes. At the same time, social constraints will be relaxed when more women, out of necessity, will join the labor force.[46]

The Gulf states economic performance might even worsen in the coming years. The 1984 economic outcome was not encouraging. The deficit in 1983–84 reached nearly $20 bn for the GCC states. The average rate of inflation was projected at 5% in 1983.[47]

Political expectations might face a difficult time as well if the Gulf States continue to ignore the demands of the people for more political participation. The oil wealth brought with it more exposure to the outside world through education, through communication and through foreigners working in the Gulf region. The governments of the Gulf states were not able to keep foreign ideas from affecting their own society. As a result, social and political strains have grown throughout the region.

Militarily, the GCC states are becoming equipped with highly sophisticated weapons and, as a result, are increasing the number of foreign personnel in the military. This increase of foreign personnel has had a two-fold effect; it has enhanced government control over its own armed forces and at the same time it has created resentment among nationals.[48]

In addition, the formation of the GCC is seen as a step towards strengthening the tribal regimes in the region. Prior to the GCC formation, Bahrain was in the process of developing more political participation. The formation of the GCC made the government more reluctant to continue the democratic experiment, and so the National Assembly was dissolved in 1975.

In conclusion, one can say that regional integration was for a long time an ultimate hope of the Gulf people; the creation of the GCC has resulted in some economic and military integration. Yet, disappointment might arise in the future if the GCC states limit their cooperation to security and economic issues and ignore the needs for social development and political participation among the six Gulf states that form the GCC.

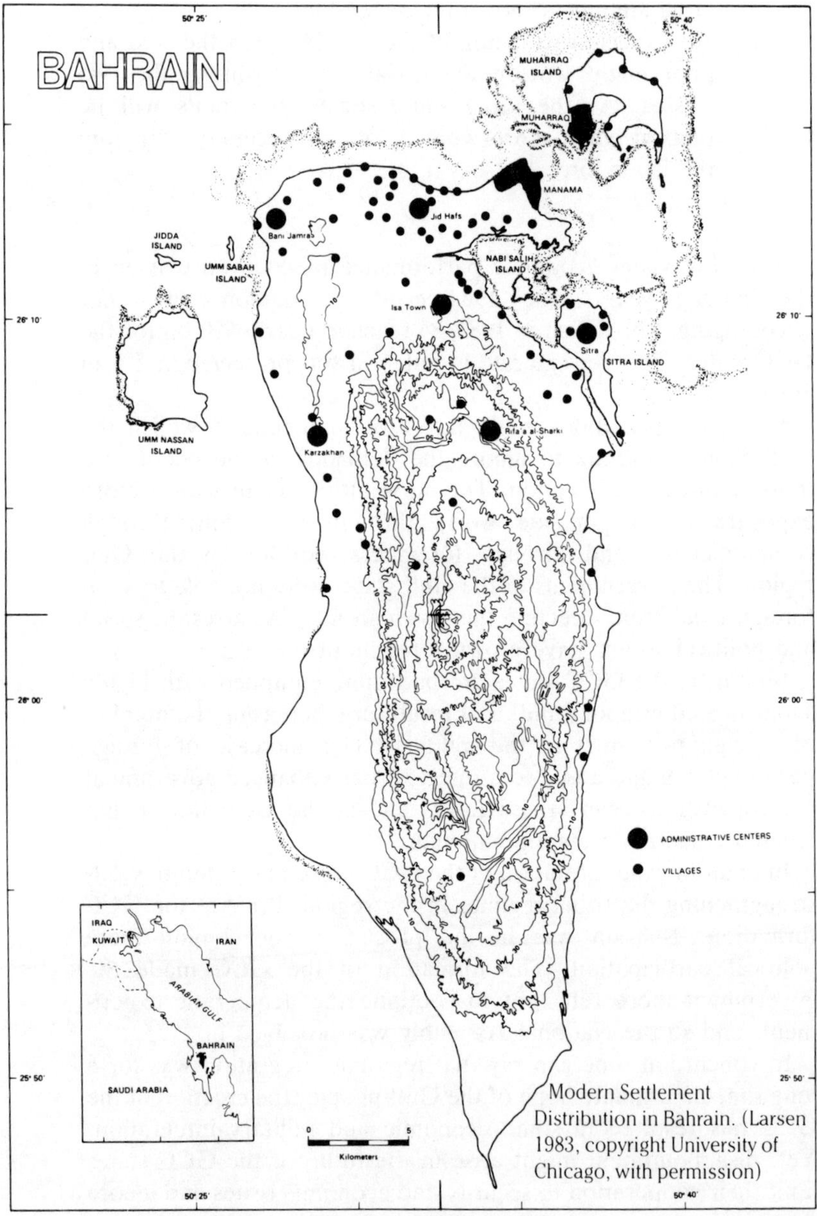

Modern Settlement Distribution in Bahrain. (Larsen 1983, copyright University of Chicago, with permission)

Map of the BAHRAIN ISLANDS

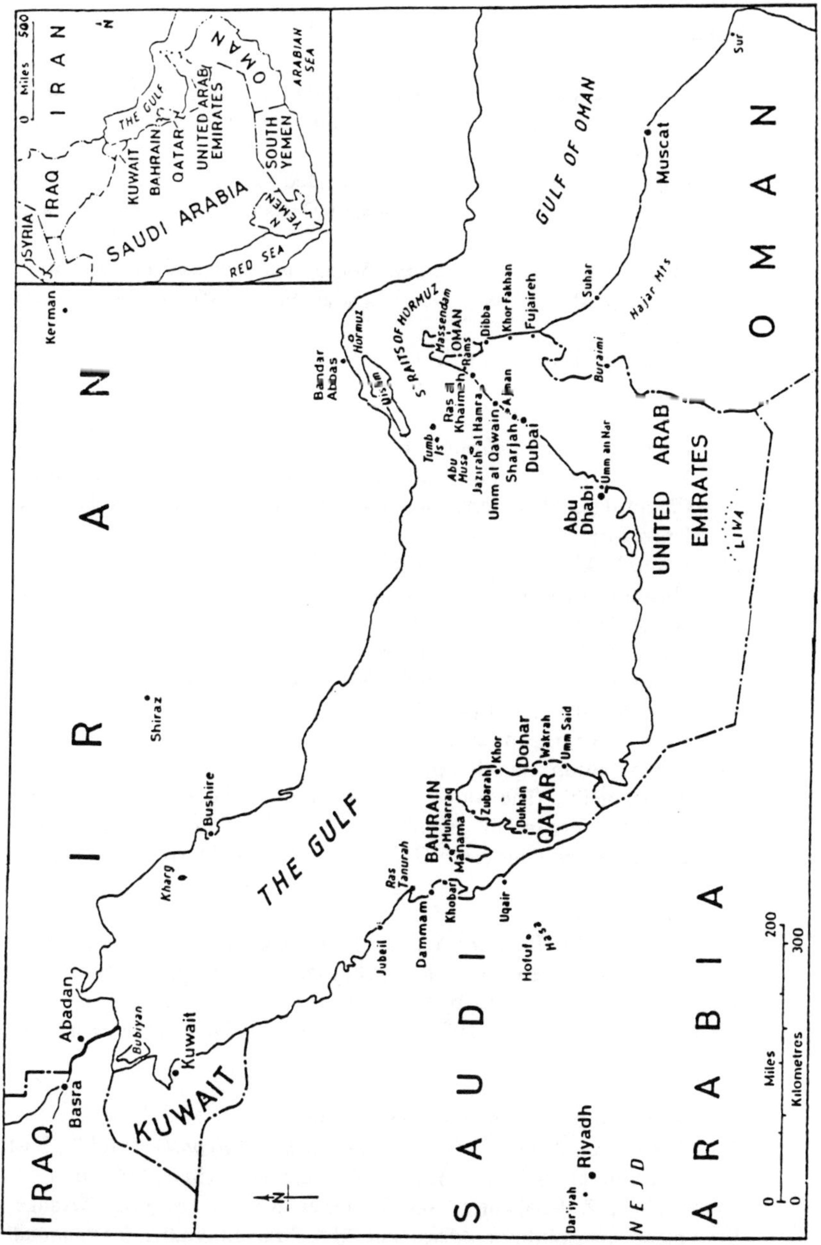

Map of the GULF COOPERATION COUNCIL (GCC)

Notes

1. Faud I. Khuri, *Tribe and State in Bahrain: The Transformation of Social and Political Authority in an Arab State*, Chicago, 1980, p. 233.
2. *Statistical Abstracts/ 1983*, Bahrain, Dec. 1984, p. 72.
3. *MEED magazine*, Oct. 1985, MEED special report on Bahrain, p. 2.
4. M. G. Al-Rumaihi, *Bahrain: Social and Political Change Since the First World War*, London and New York: Bowker, 1976, pp. 26–7.
5. Foud Khuri, op cit., p. 141.
6. Ibid., p. 99.
7. Ibid., p. 110.
8. Emile Nakhleh, *Bahrain*, Mass.: Lexington Books, 1976, p. 78.
9. Nadav Safran, *Saudi Arabia: The Ceaseless Quest for Security*, Cambridge, Mass. and London: The Belknap Press of Harvard University, 1985, p. 135.
10. Emile Nakhleh, op. cit., p. 111.
11. Hussein Sirriyeh, *US policy in the Gulf 1968–1977, Aftermath of British Withdrawal*, London: Ithaca Press, 1984, pp. 229–30.
12. Emile A. Nakhleh, op. cit., p. 77.
13. Abdul-Hadi Khalaf, 'Labor Movements in Bahrain', *MERIP Reports* (May 1985) pp. 24–5.
14. Faud I. Khuri, op. cit., p. 225.
15. Nadav Safran, op. cit., p. 268.
16. M. Rumaihi, 'The Mode of Production in the Arab Gulf Before the Discovery of Oil', in Niblock, Tom (Ed.), *Social and Economic Development in the Arab Gulf*, New York: St. Martin's Press, 1980, p. 50.
17. Ibid., p. 51.
18. M. Rumaihi, *Bahrain: Social and Political Change Since the First World War*, New York: Bowker London, 1976, pp. 49–50.
19. Faud Khuri, op. cit., p. 136.
20. *Middle East Review/1985*, World Almanac Publications, England, 1985, p. 77.
21. *MEED Magazine* (21 Sept. 1985) p. 22.
22. *Middle East Review/1985*, op. cit., p. 78.
23. Joe Stork, 'Prospects for the Gulf', *MERIP Reports*, (Middle East & Information Projects), no. 132, New York (May 1985) p. 4.
24. Mahnaz Z. Ispahani, 'Alone Together: Regional Security Arrangements in Southern Africa and the Arabian Gulf', *International Security* (Spring 1984) p. 176.

25. *Middle East Digest*, 28 (45), (9 Nov. 1984) pp. 2–4.
26. Mahnaz Z. Aspahani, op. cit., p. 161.
27. Emile Nakhleh, 'Political Participation and the Constitutional Experiment in the Arab Gulf: Bahrain and Qatar', in Niblock, Tom (Ed.), op. cit., p. 163.
28. Ibid., p. 175.
29. Mahnaz Z. Ispahani, op. cit., p. 171.
30. Joe Stork, 'Prospects for the Gulf', *MERIP Reports* (May 1985) p. 5.
31. J. E. Peterson, 'Defending Arabia: Evolution of Responsibility', *Orbis* (Autumn 1984) p. 484.
32. Thomas L. McNaugher, 'Arms and Allies on the Arabian Peninsula', *Orbis* (Autumn 1984) p. 502.
33. *Middle East Review/1985*, op. cit., p. 78.
34. Joe Stork, op. cit., p. 6.
35. John Bulloch, *The Gulf: A Portrait of Kuwait, Qatar, Bahrain and the UAE*, London: Century Publication, 1984, p. 4.
36. Lubna Al-Kazi, *The Impact of Education on Women's Economic Participation: A Case Study of Kuwaiti Women*, Paper presented to the Regional Planning Conference for Arab Women, Nicosia, Cyrpus, (24–29 June 1985). Organized by the Institute of Women's Studies in the Arab World, Beirut, Lebanon, 1985.
37. Nesta Ramazani, 'Arab Women in the Gulf', *The Middel East Journal*, vol. 39, no. 2 (Spring 1985) p. 270.
38. *The Middle East Magazine* (Oct. 1985) p. 7.
39. Nesta Ramazani, op. cit., p. 260.
40. *Al-Yamama*, 32 (791) (Saudi Arabia), (22 Feb. 1984) pp. 74–78 (Arabic).
41. Linda Soffan, *The Women of The United Arab Emirates*, London: Croom Helm; New York: Barnes & Noble Books, 1980, p. 80.
42. Shaikha al-Misnad, *The Development of Modern Education in the Gulf*, London: Ithaca Press, 1985, p. 38.
43. Abeer Abu-Saud, *Qatari Women, Past and Present*, Harlow, Essex: Longman, 1984, p. 174.
44. Eliyahu Bergman, 'The Rise and Fall of Arab Oil Power', *Middle East Review*, vol. XVIII, no. 1 (Autumn 1985) p. 6.
45. M. G. Al-Rumaihi, *The Expected Social and Psychological Impact on the Arab World of the Fall in Oil Prices*, paper presented to the symposium on 'Arabs Without Oil', organized by Arab Research Centre, London (25–26 June 1985) p. 20.
46. Ibid., p. 20.
47. *The Middle East Economic Digest*, 28 (1), 1984, p. 4.
48. Thomas L. McNaugher, op. cit., p. 524.

Chapter Three

The Present Situation of Women in Bahrain

> Men have authority over women because Allah has made the one superior to the other, & because they spend their wealth to maintain them. 4:34
> As for those wives from whom you fear disobedience, admonish them and send them to beds apart and beat them. Then if they obey you, take no further action against them. 4:34
> Marry of the women, who seem good to you, two, three, or four, & if ye fear that ye cannot do justice to so many then one only. 1:3
>
> (Holy Qur'an)

Women in Bahrain constitute nearly half the national indigenous population (49.7%) and (33.8%) of the total population including foreigners.

Women's status in Bahrain cannot be given one classification. It varies greatly according to the section of society to which women belong and the degree of education they acquire. Women who come from rich families have a life style relatively comparable with that of women in Europe; some urban women have access to work, but few have reached high managerial positions. On the other hand, women who belong to rural traditional families are the ones who suffer most from traditions, and from dominant fathers who tend to keep their daughters from attending school.

What characterizes the Gulf societies is the fostering of separate societies for men and women – a system that outlaws women from public activities and confines them to their homes. But Bahrain differs from the rest of the Gulf states on that matter. Bahrain has always been open to new ideas and the people have been noted for their relatively enlightened attitude in comparison with that of the other Gulf states. However, some traditional values are still dominant and favor separate roles for men and women and a slower pace of development in regard to women's issues. In education, for example, although females experience a great increase in educational achievement between 1971 and 1981, they still remain less educated than males. Females constituted 46% of total enrollment both at the primary and secondary levels in 1981.

As for education in general, many positive developments have emerged: in 1978/79 females formed 35.5% of the total student body (65,368). This percentage kept increasing until it reached 47.4% of the total student body (78,797) in 1983/84. During the 1980–81 academic year, a total of 1,868 students were enrolled in the Gulf College for Technology and in Bahrain University College. In 1986 the two colleges merged to form Bahrain University. The Gulf University, established in 1983 and financed by the Gulf states, is taking an important lead in education in Bahrain. In addition, higher education abroad is available for both sexes, and more than 2,600 Bahraini students were enrolled in foreign and Arab Universities during 1981. In 1983/84, the number of students studying abroad reached 879 females and 1,465 males; this was a relative decrease from 1981 because higher education was available in Bahrain in recent years.

The Ministry of Labor and Social Affairs has provided some limited social programs for females; one of these programs is the Productive Family Project, which covers 409 families, providing participants with opportunities to acquire various skills, including sewing and handicrafts. Another project is the training of local leaders. This project trains nearly 60 participants from different villages and towns who serve as a liaison between the Ministry of Labor and Social Affairs and the local people by directing them to the proper services.

CHARACTERISTICS OF FAMILIES IN BAHRAIN

Females in Bahrain, like those in the rest of the Moslem countries, exhibit a high fertility rate. In 1971 the fertility rate per female was 3.96. This high rate had decreased in 1981 to nearly 3.2,[1] a figure still considered very high even if it is compared to the average fertility rate of the Moslem countries, which is 3.3.

Table 3.1 *Percentage Distribution of Divorcees by Age Groups (1977, 1979, 1981, 1983)*

Age groups	Divorced Husband				Divorced Wife			
	1977	1979	1981	1983	1977	1979	1981	1983
Under 15	—	—	—	—	2.49	1.15	1.22	0.24
15–19	5.26	4.41	2.70	2.14	34.90	33.52	28.86	22.10
20–24	25.21	26.82	26.80	22.80	23.82	27.59	31.70	40.38
25–29	20.50	19.92	25.30	30.64	9.97	14.18	16.00	16.39
30–34	8.03	14.75	14.60	15.19	5.26	8.04	9.35	9.74
35–39	8.59	8.62	8.50	9.50	7.48	5.94	3.93	4.51
40–44	8.31	8.24	5.60	6.26	4.99	3.45	3.52	2.38
45–49	8.59	5.75	4.20	3.56	3.88	2.30	2.17	2.38
50+	13.59	11.30	12.00	9.98	5.54	3.06	2.71	1.66
Not Stated	1.94	0.19	1.10	0.24	1.66	0.77	0.54	0.24
Total	100.0	100.0	100.0	100.0	100.0	100.0	100.0	100.0
Number	331	522	738	521	331	522	738	421

Sources: Statistical abstracts 1983, op. cit., derived from Table 80, p. 114

Such a high fertility of females restricts them to marital roles and prevents them from seeking higher education, economic independence and participation in public life. The high fertility rate could be attributed to many factors such as the improvement in health services, early marriages, polygamy and the traditional ideal of a large family.

Life expectancy continues to show an increase in Bahrain. Data from the 1971 census revealed a life expectancy of 56.8 years for males and of 60.3 years for females. In 1981, life expectancy had increased to 63.6 years for males and 67.8 years for females. The increase in life expectancy could be related to the free medical services, to the spread of health centers in urban and rural areas, to the recent increase in income levels and to the improvement of living conditions in general.

Divorce rates have been increasing dramatically in the last few years (Table 3.1). In 1977, the number of divorce cases for males was 331; in 1979 it increased to 522 and kept increasing until it reched 738 cases in 1981. The same number of cases was recorded for females in the same years. In 1984, the total number of marriages by Bahrainis reached 2,535 whereas divorces reached 696. This means that the divorce rate was 20% of the total marriages in that year. This is considered relatively high for a Moslem country like Bahrain, but is considered moderate by Western standards where the divorce rate reached as high as 50% in Europe and 31% in the United states.

Polygamy, or the right of a man to marry more than one wife at the same time, is not as common in Bahrain as in the other Gulf states. The 1981 census reveals that out of 37,793 married Bahraini males, there are 2,046 who are married to more than one wife.[2] Most of those married to more than one wife are illiterate and live in rural areas.

Rural women in Bahrain lag far behind urban women in many aspects of life. Such differences are best illustrated by a study conducted by the United Nations in 1977 that looked into the situation of women in villages and their needs.[3] This study was done on a random sample of 500 women who lived in villages. The study adopted three models: the agricultural model, the fishing model and the handicraft model. Within each occupational model, the study selected a sample from different villages representing Sunni and Shi'a sects in order to have both sects within each model. However, all in the agricultural model were Shi'a. The findings of the study showed that the people in the agricultural model were opposed to the education of girls; only boys were sent to school. These people were found to be conservative in outlook and had traditional values that were obstacles to the education of women. The handicraft and industrial model covered six Sunni and Shi'a villages. People in this model produced pottery, did basket weaving and made textiles. The attitude towards the education of women was very encouraging in this model compared with that found in the agricultural model. This reflects the influence of the type of occupation on social aspects of community life. All the villages lacked recreational services except for clubs, which were available for men only. Women were not accepted as members or even allowed to participate in any of the social activities. The fishing model also covered both sects in six villages. Awareness of family planning and the education of women was evident in some Sunni villages.

It appeared that there were similarities between the villages included in the three models in terms of material resources, and social and economic services, but on the human side, there are some differences in attitudes and in readiness to accept new things, apart from the desire to have projects. The handicraft and fishing villages were found to be more positive, whereas the agricultural model displayed greater conservatism. This may be taken as an indicator of the affect of occupations on the social structure of the village and family.

In the sample studied, family size ranged from 5 to 15 persons. And over a third of the sample came from two-wife families. (Some wives live with the other wive; others have separate homes.) The study also showed that marriage was at a very early age in villages, but with some differences between the three models: in the agricultural model, 92% in the sample married before 15, compared with 77% in the handicraft model. Within each model, the marriage age was relatively younger in the Shi'a than in the Sunni villages. Marriage with relatives was very high in the three models and was higher in Shi'a than in Sunni villages. Of all the women in the three models 94% were illiterate. When they were asked about their work possibilities in their villages, more than half the sample said that women were not allowed to work outside their homes. The majority of the sample agreed that their daughters could work as teachers. The education field may have been most desired because it is the safest field in the sense that it does not mix the two sexes.

SOCIAL CHARACTERISTICS OF WORKING WOMEN

The increasing rate of women's participation in the labor force is expected to affect family life mainly by delaying marriage and reducing the number of children. The general fertility rates in Bahrain already witnessed a decrease from 3.96 in 1971 to 3.2 in 1981. As a large majority of females who enter the labor force are in the peak of the fertility age group, 20–29 years of age, it is expected that they would limit the number of their children and this has occurred in many other countries.

The most recent field study on the social and economic conditions of women in the labor force covered 1,130 families of a total of 33,884 families registered in the 1981 census (nearly 1 out of 30 of the total families in Bahrain).[4] The section on women and work discusses women in the labor force in general and the social characteristics of females in the labor force. The study has shown that the percentage of working females aged

Table 3.2 *Distribution of females, in–out of the labor force (16 years and over) by educational level*

Highest Educational Level	Illiterate	Read and Write	Elementary	Intermediate	High School	Diploma	University Degree	Unknown	Total %	Total Number
Employed	12.4	2.5	7 4	5.9	42.6	19.3	9.9	—	100.0	202
Housewife	66.9	13.9	8.6	5.2	4.9	0.3	0.2	—	100.0	1162
Student	4.1	10.3	17.6	39.3	26.2	2.4	—	—	100.0	290
Unemployed Looking for Job	—	7.1	—	11.9	78.6	—	2.4	—	100.0	42
Unemployed Not Looking for Job	—	37.5	6.2	31.2	25.0	—	—	—	100.0	16
Handicapped	97.0	3.0	—	—	—	—	—	—	100.0	76
Beggar	—	50.0	50.0	—	—	—	—	—	100.0	2
Not Stated	37.0	6.1	18.2	12.1	12.1	—	—	—	100.0	66
Total %	49.4	11.5	9.8	11.1	14.2	2.6	1.2	0.2	100.0	—
Total (number)	915	214	181	205	264	49	23	3	100.0	1854

Sources: 'Al-Awdha' Al-Iqtisadeyyah Wal-Ijtima'eyyah Lilmar'A Al-Bahraineyyah (social and economic condition of women in Bahrain), op. cit., derived from Table 3, p. 147. (Arabic)

20–24 years reached 42.6%; whereas working females aged 25–54 was 50.5%.[5] Such statistics reveal that the phenomenon of working females is recent and that the majority of females in the labor force are very young, unlike those in the Western countries, in which the labor force participation rate for females aged 25–54 is very high. In the German Democratic Republic, they constitute 87%, in Hungary 75%, in Sweden 70% and in the United Staets they constitute 60% of that age group.[6]

The study also showed that there was a positive relationship between the female educational level and the degree of their employability (Table 3.2): only 85% of working females in the sample had acquired an elementary level of education or higher, 12.4% were completely illiterate whereas only 2.5% could barely read or write. Furthermore, 73% of those who work acquired a secondary educational level or higher. This indicates that

Table 3.3 *Distribution of employed and unemployed females by age and marital status*

Age Group	Not Married	Married	Divorced	Widow	Total %	Total Number
15–19	11.5	0.0	0.0	0.0	5.5	2
20–24	64.4	22.7	30.0	0.0	42.0	92
25–29	22.1	40.2	30.0	12.5	30.1	66
30–34	1.9	15.5	20.0	0.0	8.7	19
35–39	0.0	14.4	0.0	25.0	7.3	16
40–44	0.0	3.1	20.0	12.5	2.7	6
45–49	0.0	3.1	0.0	37.5	2.7	6
50–54	0.0	1.0	0.0	12.5	0.9	2
Not Stated	0.0	0.0	0.0	0.0	0.0	—
Total %	100.0	100.0	100.0	100.0	100.0	
Total number	104	97	10*	8*	—	219

Sources: Al-Awdha' Al-Iqtisadyah Wal-Itjima'iyah Lilmar'a al-Bahrainyah (Social and economic conditions of women in Bahrain), op. cit., derived from Table 9, Chapter 3, p. 157. (Arabic)

* Numbers are too small for significance.

education is an important factor in female employability. Such a relationship becomes more evident when looking at those unemployed who were looking for jobs: nearly 80% of them have a high school diploma or higher, whereas only 56% of those unemployed, who were not looking for jobs, have acquired elementary education. Moreover, two-third of the housewives in the sample were illiterate whereas 14% could barely read and write.

The study also revealed that 47.5% of those employed or looking for jobs were not married; 44.3% were married, and the rest (8.2%) were divorced or widowed. This shows that marital status is not an important issue for female employability, despite the fact that the percentage of married females over 30 in the labor force showed a sharp decrease (Table 3.3).

Nearly two-third of the females in the sample work in the public sector, 20% work in the private sector, and 8% are self employed (Table 3.4). The public sector is characterized by a

Table 3.4 *Distribution of workers (16 years and over) by employment status and sex*

Employment Status	Males	Females	Total %	Total Number
Employer	5.9	—	5.2	79
Self-employed	19.7	7.9	18.1	278
Government Employee	48.9	69.3	51.6	791
Employee of Private Company	24.7	19.8	24.0	368
Paid Servant	0.1	1.5	0.3	4
Unpaid Servant	0.2	—	0.2	3
Not Stated	0.5	1.5	0.6	9
Total %	100.0	100.0	100.0	—
Total (Number)	1330	202	—	1532

Sources: Al Awda' Al-Iqtisadeyah wal-Ijtimaeyah Lilmar' al–Bahraineyah (social and economic conditions of women in Bahrain), op. cit., derived from Table 12, p. 160.

Table 3.5 *Distribution of females by work and number of children (under 5 years)*

Employment Status	0	1	2	3	4	Total %	Total Number
Working	8.3	17.4	9.9	5.7	—	11.1	111
Not Working	90.4	80.9	89.2	92.9	100.0	87.5	876
Not Stated	1.4	1.6	1.0	1.4	—	1.4	14
Total %	100.0	100.0	100.0	100.0	—	100.0	
Total Number	417	304	203	70	7	1001	

Sources: Al-Awdha' Al-Iqtisadeyah Wal-Ijtima'eyah Lilmar'a Al-Bahraineyah (social and economic conditions of women in Bahrain), op. cit., derived from Table 17, p. 169. (Arabic)

shorter working day than the private sector: this makes it easier for females, especially those with children, to manage both their office work and housework. Although working in the public sector is not rewarding financially, it is a secure job.

Finally, the study has shown that out of 1,001 women with children, only 11.1% work (Table 3.5). Females who left their jobs cited the main causes as their husbands' objection and having to care for the children. This indicates that child bearing and child care is an important factor affecting women's work. Women have had to withdraw from work to fulfill these roles.

WOMEN'S ASSOCIATIONS AND THEIR ROLE IN DEVELOPMENT

Labor unions and formal political parties are banned in Bahrain, and so political activities are taking place in religious centers and in cultural and sports clubs.[7] More than a hundred clubs and societies exist in Bahrain. Their functions cut across the entire social and cultural spectrum of the society. They play an important role performed by political parties in other political systems, i.e. that of representing the interests of people and of recruiting leaders.[8]

Women's voluntary associations, like men's cultural, sports, and professional associations, are considered as centers of political activity. They reflect the social and political changes that have taken place in Bahrain. They also represent a new social force that might be developed to bring about changes in the future. In addition to the five women's associations, women in Bahrain are joining other associations in great numbers. More women are joining professional organizations including those of law, engineering and social science. In recent years, more young females have joined different sport clubs, whereas in the past membership was restricted to males.

In the following section, I will limit my discussion to the five women's associations and will examine the activities that have been taking place since 1955 when the first woman's association was established in the Gulf region.

1. *An Nahdah Association*. This association was established in 1955 by a wealthy merchant who donated a piece of land and financed the building of the association over which his wife presided for many years. The association is considered the first of its kind in the Gulf region. It confined its activities to cultural and educational programs such as eradicating illiteracy, opening a day-care facility for the children of working mothers, raising the awareness of women in general and conducting research on issues such as illiteracy and divorce problems.

   Since its establishment in the 1950s, the association has had a limited membership. However, in the early 1970s, a large number of educated young females joined the association and, through legal elections, they took over and started to change the association's policy into a more radical one, pressing for social change and becoming more involved in social and political activities.
2. *Awal Association*. This association was established in 1970 in Muharraq city and consists of 240 members. It subscribes to a policy similar to that of the An-Nahdah association. Most of its members are young working females. It is concerned mostly with such activities as organizing cultural and educational programs; for example, it has opened a day-care service in some literacy centers to take care of children of females who have joined the literacy classes. Members of the society are known to be committed to the work of their society

and are more involved in political and social activities. They also believe that women should have the same rights and responsibilities as men.

3. *Child and Mother Welfare Association*. This association was established in 1960 and consists of nearly 300 members who belong to the rich merchant families and the ruling Al-Khalifa family. Most of the members are housewives. The association is funded heavily by rich individuals and private establishments. This has made it more capable of establishing different projects including the Amal Institution for the handicapped, six kindergartens and one nursery school. In addition, the association runs programs to teach women new skills such as sewing and handicrafts. Politically, the society is composed of women who are direct beneficiaries of the current political system. Most of them are related to influential and wealthy people in Bahrain; therefore, the society's commitment to political issues, such as women's political and civil rights, is more moderate than that of the previously mentioned two societies (An-Nahdah and Awal).
4. *Rafa' Cultural and Charity Association*. Established in 1970 in Rafa' city, this association concentrates on cultural programs and charity work in addition to running three kindergartens.
5. *International Women Association*. Established in 1975, this is considered the only association that includes foreign females among its members. Most of its activities consist of charity work and of other humanitarian projects such as visiting patients in hospitals.

All of the above associations are located within the main cities. However, rural women are not allowed to form their own associations. In 1979, nearly 60 young females living in rural areas asked the government's permission to establish 'Fatat Al-Reef Association', but their request was rejected. At the same time, other existing associations were not permitted to open branches in villages to accommodate new members, nor were those young females allowed by their families to travel to distant, pre-existing associations. The case of Fatat Al-Reef association is still under debate in different organizations, who feel that the authorities have started to be cautious of female associations.

The recent history of women's associations indicates that such groups, if given the chance to act, could add to the political pressure and would call for social and political change. In 1972, women's associations played an active role during the Constitutional Assembly elections, thus adding to the political tension. The Constitutional law restricted voting to males only. A few days prior to the elections, representatives from Awal, An-Nahdah and Rafa' associations presented the following petitition to the Emir of Bahrain concerning women's political rights. The following is a translation of the petition.[9]

> We, the undersigned, the popular societies that represent women in Bahrain, in order to underline the democratic laws and principles that should have been included in the election laws of the Constitutional Assembly, whose tasks will be to produce a constitution for the country, submit to the Council of Ministers our protest of the decision to deny women the right to participate in the nomination and election process. Bahrain has always been the cultural, social and civilizational leader in the Gulf; why does it today remove an active segment of its population from participation in the march toward progress? The decision to keep women away from the formation of the Constitutional Assembly and the discussion of the Constitution is the most severe insult that can be given to women, who have raised generations and who have exerted every effort over the centuries in the service of their country. Today for little reason they are removed from the political scene.
>
> The two reasons given for depriving women of their political rights (which are not at all valid) may be summarized as follows:
>
> 1. Women are veiled, and therefore it is difficult to ascertain their identity.
> 2. Women are uneducated, and therefore they have no independent opinion, so that men can influence their votes.
>
> We believe both reasons are unconvincing. As to the first, procedures may be taken to ascertain the identity of veiled women, and as to the second, a large percentage of ignorant men also exist – men who have no independent opinions. The election laws do not require that men must be aware and

> knowledgeable before they are given the right to vote. Legally the United Nations Charter clearly prohibits discrimination on the ground of sex in the area of public human rights. The Universal Declaration of Human Rights, adopted by the United Nations General Assembly in 1952, also grants men and women equal political rights.
>
> In this region, Arab societies, who face such difficulties, have recognized women's suffrage, as do many African constitutions. Today, when we demand in the name of Bahraini women that you review this decision, we are acting in accordance with a long tradition of participation of Bahrain's women in the cultural, social and political affairs of the country. As an example, we met the United Nations Special Representative, and to him we insisted on the Arabism of Bahrain.
>
> In the name of the women of Bahrain, who have had a tradition of education for over 50 years, we present this petition, hoping it will produce positive results. Women's humanity is inseparable from the whole human kind, and we believe that on the day when justice against women is eradicated, Bahrain will reassert its belief in freedom, democracy and equality in human rights and responsibilities.

The previous letter shows how women's associations in Bahrain attempted to play a larger part in the social and political events of the 1970s. At present, no associations are allowed to hold meetings or sponsor programs before they are officially licensed by the Ministry of Labor and Social Affairs. With the growing influence of the Islamic groups and the establishment of the Gulf Cooperation Council, women's associations were forced, by various laws, to limit themselves to a few local charitable activities.

Furthermore, a committee for women's affairs was trying to establish itself in 1980, and representatives of different ministries and women's associations were named. The main action of the committee was initially to increase awareness of women's needs and of their potential, and further to evaluate the advancement of women in such areas as employment, health and education in different ministries, as well as in public and private sectors. In 1981, the Committee was dissolved by the government and women's efforts were fragmented. Today, one could say that women's associations are formed either of groups of women from the upper classes seeking outlets for their charitable social inclinations or groups of young working women unable to play anything but a limited role in social change.

Impact of Women's Employment on Family Life

Prior to the oil discovery, women in Bahrain were veiled, and their role was mainly restricted to the home and child bearing. Only the wives of fishermen and peasants worked outside the home. Their work was mainly in cleaning and selling fish or in helping their husbands in the fields and in marketing products.[10] With the new economic order and the expansion of education, women's roles began to change. Such change has been more visible in urban women than in those in villages or in the poorer sectors of society, where women are still veiled and confined to their homes.

At present, female employment is expected to have a greater impact on family life, since the majority of working women are at the peak of their fertility age group (20–29 years of age). The fertility rate has already decreased from where it used to be a decade ago, when it reached its high point of 3.96 before it fell to 3.2 in 1981.

The effect of the growing rate of female employment must be noted. There is an ever-increasing negative attitude towards women's participation in the labor force. Such attitudes can be seen even in the industrialized countries. The recent increase in the participation of females in the labor force is viewed by some observers as contributing further to family stress and disorganization: children are inadequately cared for or supervised while mothers work; family routines are disrupted; working women with independent incomes are more likely to dissolve unsatisfactory marriages; and changes in women's roles inevitably lead to changes in men's roles or to conflicts.[11]

However, similar arguments are often used by many writers in Moslem and Arab countries to oppose the integration of women into the labor force. The argument goes further by stressing the fact that women in the Gulf states, as in other developing countries, are not educated or trained sufficiently to hold any jobs. Moreover, there will be no one to care for the children except foreign nannies who come mostly from such countries as India, Pakistan, Sri Lanka and the Philippines.

Another factor that has added to the problem is the inadequacy and the scarcity of day-care centers and nursery schools. This makes it very hard for many working mothers to enroll their children in such facilities. In addition, working mothers have faced another problem: the diminishing role of the extended family in which mothers, unmarried sisters or aunts used to take care of the children. The emergence of the nuclear family has not been accompanied by the provision of day-care and recreational facilities as a substitute for the traditional family.

Some critics stress that the new role of working wives and mothers may strain the husband's sense of status and identity. Moreover, a busy wife cannot provide the same level of devotion to her husband and children that a full-time housewife can. Such arguments are always used by critics of working females. However, it can be argued that there are many advantages to women working, and the most important one is the financial gain for the women as well as for the entire family. A second income for the family provides the husband and children the opportunity to have more choices in their life and to avoid many sources of anxiety brought about by smaller incomes. In addition to providing additional income, women's employment would eventually lead to a delay of marriage, a reduced birth rate and finally to more equality between the sexes.

The growing number of foreigners employed as domestic help and nannies and the disintegration of the extended family are the most important issues that are still under debate in Bahrain. Some critics are blaming these recent developments on women's changing role in society. These two topics must therefore be discussed in more detail.

THE GROWING NUMBER OF FOREIGNERS EMPLOYED AS DOMESTIC HELP AND NANNIES

Seeking outside help to do the housework or to take care of children is not a recent phenomenon. Affluent families in Bahrain used to hire local people and slaves to do such work in the pre-oil society. (This was before slavery was legally banned by the British in 1926.) After the discovery of oil, a larger section of society was affluent enough not to have to be exploited in this way. At the same time, the need for domestic help and nannies has been increasing, especially within the last decade. The solution has been to import foreign help from Asian countries, where poverty leads some women to accept jobs offering only the minimum wages, uncertain and long hours with inadequate paid leave and few social benefits.

The recent increase in the amount of foreign domestic help has created some confused reactions in Bahrain and in the rest of the Gulf states. Thousands of foreign female workers, most of them Asians, came to the region to work as housemaids and nannies. In Bahrain alone, their number reached 3,225 whereas Bahraini maids numbered only 65 in 1981.[12] The number of maids is relatively large when compared with the entire number of Bahraini families, 33,831, as recorded in the 1981 census. Much blame has been placed on working women for such an increase in nannies, which, critics claim, will lead to the disintegration of the family unity and will create a generation of children alienated from their culture, thus causing them to lose ties with their own religion and heritage.

The issue has been widely discussed in the Gulf states and has been covered by the media for a long period. Many research projects and field studies have been published, most of the finding that the magnitude of the problem has reached an alarming point and that something should be done to save future generations from losing their identity and cultural heritage. Furthermore, nannies have been blamed for the recent increase in divorce rate in Bahrain. Most of the studies have suggested that women be confined to their traditional roles as housewives and mothers as a solution for such a problem.

However, working women are not the only ones who hire foreign housemaids. In a field study conducted by the Ministry of Labor and Social Affairs on 'the effect of foreign nannies upon families in Bahrain', the data showed that only 32% of the sample who hire nannies are working women, the rest of the sample (68%) being housewives.[13]

This trend in the growing number of domestic servants is viewed by some as a characteristic feature of countries at an intermediate stage of economic development. The whole domestic sector grows with economic development, and, at the same time, tends to become more exclusively feminine.[14] Thus, the increase in foreign domestic help and nannies in Bahrain should not be viewed as an isolated problem by itself, but rather as part of the overall increase in foreign labor in Bahrain and the Gulf states, as a consequence of present economic development. There is no immediate solution for such a problem. The real solution would come with careful planning of many issues affecting family life. Among those issues are the following: more adequate child-care facilities, a smaller number of children, reforms in family laws, and finally, a change in sex-role relations that will lead to more equitable roles in the sharing of household responsibilities.

THE EMERGENCE OF THE NUCLEAR FAMILY

The recent economic development in Bahrain and the Gulf states has led to a gradual disintegration of the extended family and to the emergence of the nuclear family. Many factors have contributed to such development: the spread of education in the last 50 years has increased the trend toward a nuclear family structure; educated working couples feel capable of bringing up their own families without interference from other members of their extended family. In addition, the government housing policy could be seen as one major factor. The rapid population growth in the last four decades has put pressure on the government to provide more housing projects for the population. The construction of Isa Town in the 1960s, followed by the building of many housing projects in different areas of the island and the recent construction of Hamad town in the 1980s, has enabled many young couples with limited incomes to move away from their extended families and live in the new facilities. In addition, the current government policy of giving loans to its employees to build their own homes further encouraged the emergence of the nuclear family.

This change in family structure has not been accompanied by a change in the role of men and women. As a result, women who joined the labor force have had to play their traditional role on the one hand, serving their husbands and having a large number of children, and on the other hand, fulfilling their new role as working women. Playing both roles without the usual help from the extended family has naturally placed great pressure on them.

The new situation created by the emergence of the nuclear

family calls for an adjustment in the roles of both sexes inside the home rather than keeping women within their traditional roles. It is undesirable, if not impossible, to turn back the clock and keep women from work outside the home. It is therefore suggested that the family evolve to meet the new needs of its members. The husband should try to change his work role and share responsibilities with his wife at home.[15]

Barriers Affecting Women's Increased Participation in the Labor Force

There are many barriers that constrain the integration of women into the labor force in Bahrain. Many barriers could be related to the cultural heritage, which includes customs and norms that force most women to remain in seclusion. These barriers are more evident in Bahrain and the Gulf states than in other Moslem countries. Statistical evidence shows that low levels of female education and employment are characteristic of most Moslem societies. Furthermore, those societies that are enforcing the traditional Islamic restrictions on women have the lowest rates of female education and employment. White states the problem in the form of a hypothesis: women's educational achievement and participation in economic activity in Moslem countries varies with the enforcement of Islamic restrictions on women.[16] White uses the legal restrictions and inequalities in inheritance, marriage, divorce, child custody, and serving as witnesses, to create a scale by which Moslem nations may be ranked. This ranking applies up to January 1974. Table 3.6 illustrates the position of 19 Moslem majority nations.

The following indicators were used to create a scale of the relative improvement in women's status in Moslem countries:

(a) The establishment of a minimum legal age for marriage.
(b) The establishment of a registration requirement for marriage.
(c) The reform of the inheritance laws.
(d) The regulation or abolition of polygamy.
(e) The abolition of men's right of unilateral divorce.
(f) The establishment of secular inheritance law to replace religious inheritance law.

Table 3.6 *Reform in restrictive laws affecting women's status (to Jan. 1974)*

Rank and Country	Minimum Marriage Age	Marriage Registration	Dissolution of Marriage	Inheritance Reform	Polygamy Regulation	Abolition of Talaq	Abolition of Polygamy	Secular Inheritance	Civil Code Replacing all Religious Law
10. Albania	+	+	+	+	+	+	+	+	+
10. Soviet Central Asia	+	+	+	+	+	+	+	+	+
10. Turkey	+	+	+	+	+	+	+	+	+
8. Tunisia	+	+	+	+	+	+	+	–	–
6. Syria	+	+	+	+	+	–	–	–	–
6. Morocco	+	+	+	+	+	–	–	–	–
6. Iraq	+	+	+	+	+	–	–	–	–
6. Iran	+	+	+	+	+	–	–	–	–
5. Egypt	+	+	+	+	–	–	–	–	–
4. Pakistan	+	+	+	–	–	–	–	–	–
4. Jordan	+	+	+	–	–	–	–	–	–
4. Indonesia	+	+	+	–	–	–	–	–	–
4. Algeria	+	+	+	–	–	–	–	–	–
4. Sudan	+	–	+	–	–	–	–	–	–
3. Libya	+	+	–	–	–	–	–	–	–
1. Afghanistan	–	–	–	–	–	–	–	–	–
1. Saudi Arabia	–	–	–	–	–	–	–	–	–
1. Yemen	–	–	–	–	–	–	–	–	–

Sources: Beck, L. & Keddie (Eds), 'Women in the Muslim World', op. cit., derived from Table 2.1, p. 60

Table 3.7 *Women's education achievement and economic activity (to 1973)*

Reform Rank	School-age Girls in School (Primary) %	Female School Enrollment (Primary) (% of Total) Enrollment)	Female School Enrollment (Secondary) (% of total) Enrollment)	Females Over 15 Literate (%)	Adult Females Economically Active Total (%)	Adult Females Economically Active Non-agricultural (%)
10. Albania	99	46	40	33	36.3	–
10. Soviet Central Asia	99	48	40	94	40.0	20.0
10. Turkey	61	41	28	28	33.4	6.68
8. Tunisia	83	55	27	18	3.0	2.61
6. Syria	57	37	24	13	5.4	0.54
6. Morocco	36	33	26	6	5.9	3.89
6. Iraq	50	29	26	6	2.3	1.73
6. Iran	44	36	33	13	8.3	6.23
5. Egypt	55	38	31	9	4.8	3.60
4. Pakistan	25	29	22	8	8.8	0.97
4. Jordan	85	43	30	16	2.6	1.72
4. Indonesia	72	45	30	27	19.0	10.00
4. Algeria	54	38	29	8	1.8	1.35
4. Sudan	21	33	23	3	26.4	3.96
3. Libya	54	29	16	4	2.7	2.24
1. Afghanistan	5	13	13	2	–	–
1. Saudi Arabia	18	28	14	–	–	–
1. Yemen (N)	1	2	1	6	–	–

Sources: Beck, L and Kiddie (Eds), 'Women in the Muslim World', op. cit., derived from Table 2.2, p. 63

(g) The secularization of all personal laws through the establishment of a civil code that is not based primarily on religion.

The countries are arranged in order of their restrictiveness on women. The countries that are most restrictive and did not have any of the above reforms were ranked at the bottom of the scale. The countries that have introduced the largest number of reforms are at the top of the scale.

White also used a similar scale to test the hypothesis that the educational achievement of women varies with the enforcement of traditional Moslem restrictions.[17] The indicators of the educational achievement of women used to test this hypothesis were the following: female elementary school enrollment as a percentage of the total elementary enrollment, female secondary school enrollment as a percentage of the total secondary enrollment, female primary school enrollment as a percentage of the total population of females of primary school age, female primary school enrollment in proportion to male primary school enrollment, the literacy of females over 15 years of age, and the ratio of adult female literacy to male literacy.[18] Table 3.7 illustrates the variation in the education indicators. The nations that are most conservative in terms of legal reforms affecting women have the lowest female enrollment at all levels and the lowest adult female literacy rates. Ideally, half the school population should be female in any area. Yet the Yemen Arab Republic was ranked at the bottom of the scale; the proportion of girls in the elementary student population reached only 2%. In Saudi Arabia the proportion of girls at the same educational level was 28%. White concluded that the analysis of the data revealed a strong statistical relationship between the variables of legal reforms and women's education. The relationship is linear; increasing reforms affecting women correspond directly with increasing female educational achievement.[19] Tables 3.6 and 3.7 also indicate that those nations that have reformed those laws most equitably and that are less restrictive to women have a higher female literacy, a higher school enrollment, and a higher rate of women in the labor force.

LEGAL REFORMS AFFECTING WOMEN IN BAHRAIN

Moslem countries can be classified into three basic groups according to their type of family law:[20]

(a) Those that follow the letter of Moslem law (Bahrain and the Gulf states).
(b) Countries that are seeking solutions to modern problems by allowing the exercise of free judgement and the re-examination of the classical justice code (Egypt, Tunisia and Iraq).
(c) Countries that have almost completely abandoned classic Muslim law and that have framed their family laws along the lines of Western countries (Turkey and Albania).

Laws regarding marriage, divorce, inheritance and child custody in Bahrain are governed by the Shari'a Islamic law. Concerning marriage, for example, Islamic law does not set an age limit for marriage. Historically, boys and girls entered marriage at early ages, and a minimum age for marriage has never been introduced in Bahrain. It is left to the father or the nearest male relative to decide when to sign the marriage contract. The 1981 census recorded 37 cases of married Bahrainis age 15 and under (36 females and 1 male). However, such statistics are not reliable because child marriage is more common in villages where girls get married at an early stage of their lives. Moreover, this practice is still recognized as legally valid because there is no minimum age for marriage.

As for polygamy, Islamic law allows men to have up to four wives at any one time. Recently, many Moslem countries have sought to restrict this practice. Only Turkey, Tunisia and the Soviet Union have prohibited polygamy altogether.[21] In Bahrain, those who are married to more than one wife account for 5.4% of the total married Bahrainis – a relatively smaller percentage than in the rest of the Gulf states.

Regarding divorce laws, the right of women to dissolve their marriage is denied to them in most Moslem countries. Reforms in divorce laws are urgently needed especially because the power of divorce is completely in the hands of the husbands. It is left to their will and conscience to decide on divorce. At the same time, divorce procedures can be conducted orally; a husband can get divorced from his wife if he says three times in succession, 'You are divorced'. Immediately after the divorce, the husband pays his wife whatever unpaid money of the dower remains. Some Moslem countries such as Tunisia, Iraq and South Yemen have made such minimum reforms including requiring divorce pronouncements to be made in court. In Bahrain, being divorced is still practised in the traditional way in cases in which there is no need of court attendance.

The custody of children is an area still in need of reform. Divorced or widowed mothers retain the custody of their children for a limited time only; then, the custody is passed into the care of the father or the nearest male relative on the father's side. However, during the mother's period of custody, which lasts until the daughter is 9 years old and the son is 7 years old, the father remains guardian of the child. In addition, the mother loses right of custody as soon as she gets married again.

Reforms in inheritance laws have been less far reaching than the rest of the reforms regarding the family. There is a clear indication in the Qur'an that the male shall take double the share of his sister.[22]

Many advancements regarding women's legal status have been achieved in a few Moslem countries such as Turkey, Tunisia and South Yemen. Other Moslem countries have arrived at partial changes in the legal status of women. In Bahrain and the Gulf states, the process of change will take a longer time. The government of Bahrain seems to be reluctant even to tackle that sensitive issue. In 1985, a committee was formed to discuss the possibility of issuing a progressive family law based mainly on Islamic principles. The committee consisted of representatives of women's associations in addition to those from other professional organizations. After a lengthy debate lasting several months, the committee submitted a rough draft of a proposed family law to the Minister of Justice, who promised to study the proposal.

As can be seen, there is a great need for reforms granting women equal rights in such areas as marriage, divorce, child custody and inheritance.

THE RETURN OF VEILING

Wearing the veil is part of Moslem female tradition that goes back in history more than fifteen centuries. Recent changes in the situation of women in the Gulf states were accompanied by the removal of the veil. The veil was considered a symbol of the long confinement suffered by women. Women in Bahrain, in the early period of this century, used to cover their faces along with their bodies in a black garment called an 'Abaya'. In the villages, the Shi'a women wore a different type of veiling called a 'meshmar', a colorful garment similar to the one Iranian women in the villages wear.

Beginning with the 1950s, women became increasingly less restrictive in covering their faces until the 1960s, when women started taking the veil off. Over the years, the number of unveiled women has increased mostly in towns. In the villages, however, few are still wearing the colorful veil; the majority of young villagers are using the black 'Abaya' instead.

Despite such an increase in the number of women who are not wearing the veil, the roots of the past lie deeper in the personality and culture of the present generation. Almost all unveiled women wear the black traditional 'Abaya' during mourning and on sad occasions. The return to veiling was viewed by many Western writers as part of the Islamic movement and as a return to the old Islamic teachings. This might be true in some respect, but one should keep in mind that sex segregation and veiling have been the norm for centuries in the Gulf region. There is no reason to expect such a deeply rooted heritage to disappear in a short period of time.

Another point that needs clarification is the type of veiling women wear in the region. There are two types of veiling in Bahrain and the Gulf states:

(a) The traditional veil consists of a black garment 'Abaya', which women used to wear whenever they went out of their homes.

(b) The more recent Islamic veil 'Hijab' consists of a piece of cloth covering the women's hair and a long dress showing only the hands and feet and is worn outside and inside the homes. This kind of veiling is not rooted in Bahraini heritage. Rather, it has been recently imported from other Arab and Moslem countries. The 'Hijab' was first worn by young students who went abroad for higher education in places where they mixed with other Arab and Moslem students representing different Islamic

> political movements and who only lately have adopted the Islamic dress. Therefore, it was seen by some as carrying a political message of protest against the establishment and its policies.

The Islamic dress cuts across classes and sects; those who wear it belong to both sects (Sunnah and Shi'a) and they also belong to different social classes ranging from the upper to the lower-middle income class.

Whatever the reasons for wearing the 'Hijab', it has been used by many to serve purposes other than religious ones. This researcher had various non-formal interviews with educated working females wearing the Islamic 'Hijab'. Their answers show that the women wear it for different purposes. A female civil engineer answered that her husband was uncomfortable seeing her working on the site with foremen and laborers; as a solution, she chose to wear the Islamic 'Hijab' in order to be able to keep her marriage and her career as well. Another educated women explained that she was wearing the 'Hijab' so that she could move freely and go to work and mix with men without causing any embarrassment to her husband and her teenage sons. Other working women gave similar answers, which indicate that the increasing number of working women has helped in the spread of the Islamic veiling, the 'Hijab'. It shows also that women's interest in joining the labor force has been much greater than the change in traditions regarding women's clothing and seclusion. What has been increasingly important to them is the development of their work skills and their consequent economic independence.

The Islamic veil is seen by some as a complex symbol that can have multiple implications and different effects. Worn for one reason, it can become a symbol for conservatism or for reaction against modernization; worn for another reason, it can become a symbol for an Islamic approach to the solutions of old problems and new problems. However it is used, it means different things to different people within the society, and it means different things to westerners than it does to Moslems living in the Middle East.[23] Others question whether the return of veiling is a setback to modernity. If modernity means unveiling, fashionable clothes, mixing freely with the opposite sex, and dating, then veiled women would represent a setback to the cause of 'modernity'. If modernity, on the other hand, means the learning of modern science, technology, and the humanities, and if it means commitment and preparation for a career outside the home, then veiled women are quite 'modern'.[24]

The return of veiling could be compared in some ways to the return of the 'Thoub', the traditional dress men wear all over the Gulf region. In the early 1950s, many educated men who graduated from different Western and Arab universities started wearing western clothes as a sign of being modern and liberal. In the 1970s, there was an increase in oil revenues, resulting in a large influx of foreign labor in the Gulf region. Following the formation of the Gulf Cooperation Council in 1981, Bahrainis began to more closely associate themselves with the rest of the Gulf people. As a result, most Bahraini men put aside western clothes and started wearing the traditional 'Thoub' in order to be easily identified as 'Khaleejis' (the original people of the Gulf) and to be distinguished from foreigners or the non-Khaleejis who have outnumbered the nationals in the last decade.

Thus, the return to veiling is more or less similar to the return of the traditional 'Thoub' by Bahraini males as a sign of identity with the Gulf people – a Khaleeji identity. The short period of westernization was not rooted in the heritage of the people; the great increase in wealth and the increase in the number of foreigners created a sense of status among the Bahraini people who wanted to be identified with the rest of the Gulf people.

The Need for a Comprehensive Family Policy

Family policy refers to a series of measures designed to support the family; it covers provisions regulating relations between individual members of the family. It could be identified as what the state does, by action or inaction, to affect people in their roles as family members or to influence the future of the family as an institution. Family policy could be defined as a field or as a perspective:[25] Family policy as a field, includes population policy and family planning, cash and in-kind transfer payment, employment, housing, nutrition and health policies. In addition, child care, child development and the whole field of social policy for women have all been defined as part of this field. As a field, family policy covers a modest domain. It included programs to be assessed, improved, dropped or added to. Family policy as a perspective or criterion for social policy choice suggests the consideration of the family's well-being. The use of such a definition for family policy is more recent; it is not seen as economic growth and national power, but as the enhancing of the quality of life and doing whatever will be required institutionally to promote a sexual equality that includes fuller participation by women in all fields of work and politics.[26]

Family policy contains both direct and indirect measures; this means everything the government does to and for the family. It covers all the planned, intended effects that aim in a complex way at influencing the living conditions and attitudes of families in order to assure that the functioning of the family will be in harmony with the requirements of overall development.

Family policy varies from one social system to another, and it is in harmony with the changing needs of the family. There is no comprehensive overall national policy in Bahrain; yet, there are many social policies relating to family concerns. Such policies include housing, education, health, food subsidy, social security, day-care services and maternity leave.

As mentioned earlier, housing policies have helped the nuclear family to form an independent household. In addition, government loans to its employees and the construction of new towns have permitted many middle-income families to obtain their own houses. The decade of the 1970s witnessed an average increase of 2,176 houses per year, far exceeding any previously recorded rate of new housing.[27]

Health policy is considered an important component of family policy. Free medical care in Bahrain and the construction of health centers in many rural and urban areas have helped to improve pre-natal and post-natal care, to increase the life expectancy for both sexes and to decrease child mortality.

Government subsidies in food prices have helped families with limited incomes. Such essential food items as meat, rice and grains were subsidized to meet the increase in prices caused by inflation.

Free schooling at all educational levels had existed in Bahrain since the beginning of this century. But young children (age 0–6 years) are still not provided with adequate and sufficient day-care and kindergartens.

The absence of family policy in Bahrain has not meant a total neglect of the needs of working mothers. Working women with young children have some benefits; for example, there is maternity leave, which lasts for 6 weeks for mothers who are being given reduced working hours (one hour per day) during the breast-feeding period.

Social insurance in Bahrain is a form of group insurance operated by a governmental organization called 'the General Commission for Social Insurance'. The insurance program helps to make up for the loss of earned income. Social insurance, in general, helps to prevent economic insecurity by pooling the contributions paid by covered earners and their employers to provide protection against the loss of earned income.[28] The coverage is compulsory, and payment is based on past earnings and contributions. Social insurance was established in Bahrain in 1976. It is considered a source of income for a large number of beneficiaries and covers retirement pensions, accidents on the job, disability, old age and death. Under social insurance, female workers retire at 55 years of age where males retire at 65.

It seems rather difficult to evaluate the social insurance program because it has been so recently established (less than a decade ago). It will take a long time for most people under this program to get effective retirement benefits because the system matures slowly. Most of the older people under this program are still working. At present, the number of beneficiaries of old age in 1983 was only 11 males and no females, whereas the number of disabled beneficiaries reached 141 males and 1 females.[29] Such numbers reflect the fact that working women are a recent phenomenon.

Labor force participation by women seems to be a long-term trend and one that is irreversible. It needs to be planned carefully without harming the family. Therefore, family policy is conceived as an instrument that should combine the labor market policy and aims at facilitating women's participation in the labor market by means of a package consisting of the legislation and programs explained below.

ESTABLISHING A PROGRESSIVE FAMILY LAW

The need for a progressive family law is enormous. Family law regulates marital patterns and relations; it also views marriage as a partnership with shared duties and obligations. In the event of a divorce, full parental rights and duties will be held by the parent who is responsible for the care and training of the child. This will improve the position of divorced wives and mothers. Maternity leaves given to working mothers are considered very short (45 days only). A longer paid leave of 6 to 8 months with no loss of status at work is needed for working mothers.

ESTABLISHING MORE DAY-CARE FACILITIES AND KINDERGARTENS

The supervision of children during a mother's absence from home because of work is another problem that needs an immediate solution. Domestic servants have made it easier for mothers to continue in their jobs, but there is some doubt that this is the best solution for a working mother. Domestic help can be a substitute for a working married woman in her housekeeping only but not in bringing up the children. (A program designed to establish day-care centers and kindergartens for children (aged 0–6 years) of working and non-working mothers is discussed in full detail in Chapter Four.)

ERADICATING THE ILLITERACY OF WOMEN AND ISSUING A LAW FOR COMPULSORY EDUCATION

Education is an essential component of female employability. In Bahrain, the illiteracy rate of females is much higher than that of males. The 1981 census showed that the number of illiterate men and women, aged 10 years and over, reached 53,239. Women formed a majority of 35,114 or nearly 66% of the total. As for the labor force, statistics indicate that illiterate female workers have less opportunity to join the labor force. (A program to eradicate female illiteracy and to issue compulsory-education legislation is discussed in detail in Chapter Five.)

INCREASING THE PARTICIPATION OF FEMALES IN CURRENT VOCATIONAL TRAINING PROGRAMS

There is an increasing demand for quality and efficiency in labor. At the same time, the percentage of the population (especially the female population) who cannot be rated as skilled workers is increasing. This could be caused by the constant rise in job requirements and by the inefficiency of current vocational training programs in Bahrain. (An assessment of current programs and proposed programs for women's vocational training will be discussed in Chapter Six.)

It is nearly impossible to ascertain the effect of the family policy measures proposed to be carried out in Bahrain; other factors always interfere and work for or against such policies. One can only predict some of the consequences. As mentioned earlier, the recognition of the economic and social necessity of women's employment should be an essential part of family policy.

Women's roles are clearly changing, but the government has to play a greater role in these changes and has to deal systematically with the question of facilitating the multiple roles for women as wives, mothers, and as workers. For example, the fate of the Women's Affairs Committee, which was formed in 1980 only to be dissolved later, should be reconsidered. A committee of this sort, along with the formation of a department for women's affairs, is needed to monitor women's activities, to conduct studies regarding women, to gather statistics on marrige, divorce, birth, to carry out research on women and the family, and to recommend the kinds of measures that should be taken in the future.

Notes

1. *Statistical Abstracts/1983*, Bahrain, Council of Ministers, Central Statistics Organization, (Dec. 1984) Table 55, p. 84.
2. *Bahrain Census of Population and Housing/1981*, Cabinet Affairs, Directorate of Statistics, Bahrain, (Nov. 1982) Table 15, p. 42.
3. *Preliminary Investigation into the Social Situation and Needs of Women in Villages in Bahrain*, United Nations Development Program, United Nations, New York, 1977, p. 2.
4. *Al-Awdha' Al-Iqtisadeyah wal-Ijtima'eyah lil-Mar'a al-Bahraineyah (dirasah mydaneyah)* (social and economic conditions of women in Bahrain), a field study, Ministry of Labor and Social Affairs, Economic Commission for Western Asia (ECWA), and the Institute for Research, Beirut, Bahrain, 1985 (Arabic).
5. Ibid., pp. 144 and 145.
6. Sheila B. Kamerman and Alfred J. Kahn, *Child Care, Family Benefits, and Working Parents: A Study in Comparative Policy*, New York: Columbia University Press, 1981.
7. Fuad Khuri, *Tribe and State in Bahrain: The Transformation of*

Social and Political Authority in an Arab State, Chicago and London, 1980, p. 154.
8. Emile A. Nakhleh, *Bahrain*, Mass.: Lexington Books, 1976, p. 143.
9. Ibid., p. 143.
10. M. G. Al-Rumaihi, *Bahrain, Social and Political Change Since the First World War*, London and New York: Bowker, 1976, p. 153.
11. Sheila Kamerman and Alfred Kahn, *Child Care, Family Benefits, and Working Parents*, New York: Columbia University Press, 1981, p. 4.
12. *Bahrain Census of Population and Housing, 1981*, Cabinet Affairs, Directorate of Statistics, Bahrain, (Nov. 1982), Table 36, p. 151.
13. *Athar Al-Murabbeyat Al-Ajnabeyyat Ala Khsa'is Al-Usrah Fil-Bahrain*, Dirasah Mydaneah (Impact of foreign nannies on the characteristics of families in Bahrain), Ministry of Labor and Social Affairs, Bahrain, 1983, p. 70 (Arabic).
14. Ester Boserup, *Women's Role in Economic Development*, New York: St. Martin's Press, 1970, p. 103.
15. Ralph Smith (Ed.), *The Subtle Revolution: Women at Work*, Washington, D.C.: The Urban Institute, 1979, p. 199.
16. Elizabeth White, 'Legal Reforms as an Indicator of Women's Status in Muslim Nations', in Lois Beck and Nikki Kiddie (Eds), *Women in the Muslim World*, Cambridge, Mass. and London: Harvard University Press, 1978, p. 53.
17. Ibid., p. 61.
18. Ibid., p. 61.
19. Ibid., p. 62.
20. Sayed Ali Raza Naqvi, 'Modern Reforms in Muslim Family Laws: a General Study', *Islamic Studies*, vol. XIII, no. 4 (Dec. 1974) p. 236.
21. Noel Coulson and Doreen Hinchcliffe, 'Women and Law Reform in Contemporary Islam', in Lois Beck and Nikki Kiddie (Eds), *Women in the Muslim World*, Cambridge, Mass. and London: Harvard University Press, 1978, p. 40.
22. Ibid., p. 47.
23. Elizabeth W. Fernea, *A Veiled Revolution: A Study Guide to the Film*, Austin: Texas University Press, 1982, p. 6.
24. Saad Eddin Ibrahim, *The New Arab Social Order: A Study of The Social Impact of Oil Wealth*, Boulder, Col.: Westview Press; London: Croom Helm, 1982, p. 19.
25. Sheila Kamerman and Alfred Kahn (Eds), *Family Policy: Government and Families in Fourteen Countries*, New York: Columbia University Press, 1978, p. 495.
26. Sheila Kamerman and Alfred Kahn (Eds), op. cit., p. 497.

27. *Social Indicators for Bahrain*, Ministry of Labor and Social Affairs, Bahrain (Dec. 1982) p. 65.
28. Robert Ball, *Social Security, Today and Tomorrow*, New York: Columbia University Press, 1978, p. 5.
29. *At-Taqreer As-sanawi lil-Hy'ah Al-Ammah Lit-ta'meenat Al-Ijtima'eyah/1983* (Annual report for Social Insurance Commission/ 1983), Bahrain, 1984, Tables 11 and 12, pp. 36 and 37 (Arabic).

Chapter Four

Child-care Services in Bahrain

> Child care services are a central family policy vehicle, a necessary response to the entry of women into the labor force, or even a precondition of such entry if the price is not too high. Child care services are also a basic response to family change and new family size.[1]

This is the first of three policy analysis chapters that explore the prerequisites for achieving the increased labor force participation of women in Bahrain. We have already stressed that there will also be a need for significant reforms in family laws to support the essential family planning innovations. The present chapter, dealing with child care, is a central component of family policy. Chapter Five on education and female employment and Chapter Six on vocational training for females, outline a family 'sensitive' approach to these essential components of the broader labor market policy we consider necessary to integrate more women into the labor force.

The entry of mothers with young children into the labor force has created great concern over the care and nurture of children whose mothers work. Questions about the upbringing of those children have caused a further controversy. In addition to the question of child care is the fear among some groups of the possible decrease in fertility rates if more women join the labor force; also of concern to some is the effect this trend would have on marriage relations (see Chapter Three).

In Bahrain, working mothers with young children joined the labor force before there were adequate child-care services. The number of those who actually enter and leave the labor market is not known because there is a lack of sufficient studies and reliable statistics on this issue. However, in a survey conducted by the Ministry of Labor and Social Affairs on 500 working women, married women formed 46% of this figure; 75% of the sample were 20–29 years old, an age range during which women usually establish their families and raise children.[2]

As in most countries, women with more children work less. A recent study of women's economic and social condition in Bahrain indicated that working mothers with children under 5 years of age have a greater tendency to leave the work force and that the number of working mothers with children under 5 decreases with the increase in the number of children in that age group. Table 4.1 shows that the percentage of working mothers with one child under 5 is 17.4%; the percentage of those who have two children under 5 decreases to 9.9% and keeps decreasing to 5.7% for those who have 3 children under 5; it reaches zero with mothers of four children under 5.

The inadequate number and poor quality of nurseries and day-care centers in Bahrain have become more critical as the number of women who have joined the labor force has increased. As some authorities in this field have noted, there is some

Table 4.1 *Distribution of women by work and the number of children under 5 years of age*

	Number of Children						
Relation to Work	0	1	2	3	4	total (%)	total (No.)
Working Women	8.3	17.4	9.9	5.7	—	11.1	111
Non-working Women	90.4	80.9	89.2	100	87.5	876	
Not Stated	1.4	1.6	1.0	1.4	—	1.4	14
Total (%)	100.0	100.0	100.0	100.0	100.0	100.0	
Total Number	417	304	203	70	7	—	1001

Sources: Al-Awdha' Al-Iqtisadeya wal-Ijtima'iya lilmar'a al-Bahraineya (social and economic conditions of women in Bahrain), op. cit., derived from Table 17, p. 169. (Arabic)

correlation between the increase of out-of-home child-care services and the increase of females in the labor force. However, it is unclear which came first.[3]

In any case, demands for child-care programs in Bahrain are growing. Such demands are largely related to the need of mothers who do wish to work outside the home to support their families. All indicators point towards an increasing need for adequate day-care facilities and nurseries over the next few years.

THE GROWING NEED FOR DAY-CARE SERVICES

Day-care services lag behind the rapid social change that has brought the need for such services. The percentage of working mothers who represent all socio-economic levels has been increasing over time. Therefore, day-care facilities are needed for those mothers who are unable to arrange for adequate child care within the home.

Servants and nannies as part-time substitutes for mothers are economically attainable in Bahrain because of the relatively low salaries received (approximately $90–100 per month), bearing in mind that the salary of a working female ranges from $600 to $2,000. The number of foreign servants and nannies could even exceed the potential demands of all working mothers. But foreign nannies are not the best educational institute for young children.

At the same time, the nuclear family is finding itself increasingly unsupported by relatives because it is not always possible for the kinship group to find homes in the same neighborhood. So the extended family is no longer available for child rearing (see Chapter Two). In addition, there is an acknowledgement by nearly all parents that the task of child-rearing is not theirs alone but should be shared by professionals and by the community as a whole.[4] This view might surprise Western readers, but is quite consistent with the system in Bahrain.

Although the primary responsibility for child care and education is closely connected with the home environment, changes in living conditions and family structure have created an increasing need to find substitute help. Out of that need, day-care nurseries were established.

Preschool programs are seen as being helpful to an increasing number of parents who work outside the home, and as a socializing agent, especially for children who have no siblings. Moreover, the supply of high quality day-care services relative to the number of chidren who will need those services is an important issue to parents who do not want to see their children placed in marginal care arrangements. At the same time, part-time employment has made child-care arrangements more flexible, but most working women have no option other than full-time work. Clearly, then, child-care needs and problems continue to be seen as a source of constant stress and as the most important issue for working mothers.

THE EFFECT OF SUBSTITUTE CARE

The effect of day care on children aged 3–5 years of age is the most sensitive issue relating to the employment of mothers. Many studies have attempted to assess the differential effect of home care versus day care on the development of the child. The evidence suggest that only a few differences have been observed between children reared at home and those raised in group-care settings. In four comparative studies on the intellectual development of children reared in day-care versus home-care situations, none found any substantial differences.[5]

Other studies have been conducted in industrial countries to measure the effects of day care on infants and toddlers. One major study is the New York City Infant Day Care Study (Golden, 1977),[6] a unique longitudinal study comparing low-income children reared at home, children with center experience, and those in family care. The study included 400 children from 32 public, private, and community-operated groups and family infant day-care programs, and from 20 preschool day-care programs. The quality of the programs ranged from excellent to poor. The major findings were remarkable; on all measures of intellectual, social and emotional functions, children attending infant day-care programs for several years did as well or better than equivalent samples of home-reared children. The study also showed that families using infant day-care programs did not appear to be greatly affected by these programs; at the completion of the study, the families who had used infant day care for several years did not differ significantly from families who had recently entered the program. Furthermore, the study indicated that no relationship emerged between the age of entry and any of the outcome measures of psychological development at 36 months. The major differences were observed between group and family programs related to nutrition and health care, rather than to psychological development. The group programs were found to be superior to family programs in providing higher quality food and health services.

Another important study was conducted by Belsky and Steinberg (1978) on the effect of day care on young children: the cognitive, emotional and social development of the child and the effect of day care on the family unit.[7] Their findings, which were drawn from 40 studies, indicated that the day-care experience has neither positive nor negative effects on the intellectual development (as measured by standardized tests) of most children. For economically disadvantaged children, however, day care may have an enduring positive effect. For children from relatively advantaged families, exposure to day care does not appear to result in any long-term gains in test performance. So, disadvantaged children may benefit from an enriching day-care experience, whereas children who come from economically advantaged families experience little positive or negative effect from such programs.

Regarding the effect of day care on the child's attachment to his mother, evidence from research offers little support for the claim that day care disrupts the child's tie to his mother. Significant disruption of the mother-child bond does not appear likely to happen especially with high quality day care. In addition, there is no indication that exposure to day care decreases the child's preference for his mother in comparison with an alternative familiar caregiver. The authors indicated also that the effects of day care on the socialization of adult-like behavior indicate that at early and later ages, there may be more peer-oriented. Some studies reviewed suggest that at earlier ages (12–18 months), day-care children in the presence of their mothers are more likely to look at and interact with peers than are matched home-reared chidren. Also, day care-reared children, when compared with age mates reared at home, interact more with peers in both positive and negative ways. However, some evidence does suggest that children enrolled in day care for extended periods of time show increased aggression towards peers and adults and decreased cooperation with adults, and more involvement in educational activities, once the child enters school.

The third important study to be discussed here is conducted by Clarke-Stewart and Fein (1983).[8] The authors made a selective review of literature on child development and practice from early childhood programs. Their findings will be summarized in the following paragraphs.

When children are placed in day care, although they continued to be attached to their mothers, there may be a difference in the quality of that relationship. These differences are in the direction of greater distance from avoidance of, or independence from mother, and they show up in mildly stressful situations with unfamiliar people in unfamiliar places. They are most likely to be extreme if day care is begun in the first year, before a secure and stable attachment to mother has formed, and they are likely to be the result of the amount of time the children spend away from mother and the amount of integration they have with other care-givers. For most children, this pattern of greater distance from mother probably reflects an adaptive reaction to a realistic appraisal of the situation rather than a pathological disturbance.

As for social development in early childhood programs, children attending these programs are more socially competent or mature. Such a social component arises from a combination of variables. It may be that children in these programs develop social competence because they are given direct instruction in social skills in a context in which peers and parental adults offer them the opportunity to practise social skills and in which independence and self-direction are allowed and encouraged.

All studies reviewed of children in day care have included some measures of the children's intellectual development and have indicated that children in day-care centers do as well as those at home.

The effect of day care on children's physical health and development varies according to the children's background. When infants or children are from poor families, being in day care advances motor development and activity and increases height and weight. For physical development, day care in either a center or a home appeared to be advantageous, but for motor development, the advantage has been found only in centers. In sum, the evidence indicates that day-care children become or continue to be attached to their mothers, but that there may be differences in the direction of greater avoidance, independence or distance from mother.

Thus, day-care programs do not cause problems, but the way in which such care is structured and supervised may. A day-care center or a day-care home can be similar to a good family in its influence on children in providing stable, warm relationships with a care-giver and encouraging social and emotional development of children. Or it can, like some family settings, destroy a child.[9]

The general view of some experts is that the discomfort is greater for the small children than for those above 3 years of age. It might be too exhausting both emotionally and physically, especially for those below the age of three, to spend most of the day in a day-care facility. In fact, few studies in recent years revealed some evidence of negative effects of day care on the development of infants. In a recent study, Belsky concludes that entry into center care in the first year of life is a risk factor for the development of insecure–avoidant attachments in infancy and heightened aggressiveness and withdrawal in the preschool and early school years.[10] Emotional adjustment of those under 3 years of age is more difficult. Also, there is a great risk of contagion from infectious diseases among the lower age group. In general, one can say that the effects of substitute care on children depend mainly on the quality of that care and on the characteristics of the child. In addition, there is a growing belief that some form of early childhood intervention might have a positive effect on a child's development. Moreover, day-care programs can free many low income mothers to take advantage of employment and training opportunities, which could then raise the standard of living of the family.

This research might apply to Bahrain as well. The premise is that children's needs are unique throughout the world, where a broad community of nations share an interest for the outcomes of improved care and education of the very young child.

RELATED EXISTING PROGRAMS IN BAHRAIN

Day-care nurseries and kindergartens in Bahrain are a relatively recent phenomena. The first day-care nursery was established in 1955. Since then, the number has kept increasing dramatically, especially in the last decade. In 1975/76, there were only 8 day-care nurseries and kindergartens with 815 children enrolled. In 1981/82 the number of facilities increased to 16, whereas the number of preschool children enrolled increased to 2005, representing 5% of the cohort aged 0–4 years. By the end of the decade (1985/86), the number increased to 64 with 5,000 children under 6 years of age enrolled. Only 8 day-care nurseries accommodate children under 3 years of age, the rest (56) are mostly for children of 3–6 years of age. In addition, there are nearly 28 kindergartens, which are part of foreign educational institutions.

Such dramatic expansion is partly attributed to the increase in the number of working women with preschool children in the last decade. It also reflects the great demand for such services for both working and non-working mothers who wish to enroll their children in such facilities. The number of preschool children under the age of six is not well known although some studies predict it is more than one-fifth of the entire population.[11] The medium projection of the population aged 0–4 years is expected to reach 53,141; the Bahraini population of the same cohort reached 41,955 or 15% of the national population.[12]

Besides the scarcity of the day-care programs, the majority of the staff are neither well-educated nor well-paid. Most administrators and teachers do not have college degrees and few have special training for such care. In a survey conducted in 1981, 4 out of 149 preschool teachers were college graduates, and the rest had an elementary and secondary level of education or only an elementary education.[13] This ratio is generally below the standard required in most industrialized countries, where a typical degree for a fully qualified kindergarten teacher is earned on the basis of a two- or three-year course after high school. In addition, child-care services in Bahrain were found to be unorganized, often unlicensed, and not uniform in quality. (They ranged from excellent to poor.) Yet these services are indispensible to a growing number of working women of child-bearing age.

There is also a discontinuity and a lack of coordination in the policy of the educational activities for preschool children in Bahrain. Day care nurseries for children age 0–3 years on the one hand, lie under the supervision and sponsorship of the Ministry of Labor and Social Affairs, whereas the kindergarten level, for children aged 3–6 years, is under the supervision of Ministry of

Education. The High Council for Youth and Sports has a special department for childhood programs and research on day-care services. The Ministry of Health has no role in supervising the health and nutrition of young children attending preschool programs. The lack of coordination and cooperation among those four departments makes it more difficult to bring about any progress in the field of child care. However, the increase in demand for child-care services in recent years has made the government become more involved and take a number of measures to stimulate and encourage the creation of day-care nurseries and kindergartens. The Ministry of Labor and Social Affairs furnishes day-care nurseries and kindergartens run by women's associations a small annual grant, an equivalent of $9,000 each.

The quality and standard of child-care services in general does not appear to be high. A field study was conducted in 1980 to assess the conditions of day care and kindergartens in Bahrain. The study described most of the 16 facilities in existence at the time as inefficient and inadequate: many were situated in old buildings, the child/adult ratio was very high and the average number of children in each class was 23.5–47. Furthermore, there were no nurses or social workers among the staff and the fees ranged between $25–80 per month.[14]

The researcher conducted an informal field study in March 1986 to update the information on child-care services (see Table 4.2). The study covered 11 day-care nurseries and kindergartens, which form 17% of the entire existing facilities with 1,356 children representing more than a quarter of the total 5,000 children enrolled at that time. The sample was selected to represent different geographical areas from all over Bahrain. The findings were as follows:

1. Children with mothers working outside the home accounted for 686 or 51% of the sample. This means that working and non-working mothers enroll their children in such facilities. However, most of those children were in kindergartens and few were in day-care nurseries.
2. Most of the facilities did not have nurses on staff. A few had some care-minders with first-aid training. Only the foreign kindergartens have state registered nurses.
3. Four out of eleven facilities investigated were built for the

Table 4.2 *Distribution of day care by location, age and number of children, number of working mothers, average number in each classs, staff and fees (1986)*

Name of School	Location	Age of Children	No. of Children (School)	No. of Children (Class)	No. of Children with Working Mothers	No. of Staff	Fees
1: Nadeen (British)	Manama	3–8 yrs	130	22	—	15	$ 350 (term)
2: Hibah	Manama	2 months–3 yrs	40	20	11	3	$ 45 (month)
3: Dar Al-hadhana	Manama	3–6 yrs	273	25	75%	23	$ 49 (month)
4: An-Nahda	Manama	3–6 yrs	150	20	54	14	$ 43
5: Dunia Al-atfal	Muharraq	3–6 yrs	31	15	2	4	$ 45
6: Bahjat Al-atfal	Muharraq	3–6 yrs	106	25	70%	10	$ 50
7: Atfal Awal	Muharraq	3–6 yrs	105	25	70	10	$ 43
8: Jannat-al-Atfal	Isa Town	1–5 yrs	58	18	40	10	$ 54
9: Majid Al-Zayani	East Rifa'	3–6 yrs	183	28	90	14	$50
10: At-tefl an-namoodhajeyah	Jed-hafs	3–6 yrs	150	25	60	13	$ 57
11: Bani-Jamra	Bani-jamra	4–6 yrs	130	26	15	13	$34

purpose of day care; the rest were built for other purposes.

4. The average number of children in each facility varied from 31 to 273 children.

In general, the existing child-care facilities could be classified into three categories according to the quality of care and services: cleanliness, staff qualifications, adult/child ratio and the quality of the physical facility.

(a) Kindergartens that are part of private (foreign and national) educational institutions are considered the best among the existing facilities. They also charge high fees, and there are 28 of them.

(b) Day-care nurseries and kindergartens run and supervised by women's associations number only 14. Their quality is poorer than (a) above in terms of adult/child ratio and staff qualifications. However, they have spacious buildings that are designed especially for the purpose of child-care use. They are also subsidized and furnished by the Ministry of Labor and Social Affairs.

(c) The rest of the day-care nurseries and kindergartens (50) are commercial and are run by private individuals. Although a few in this category could be considered as good as (a) and (b) above, the majority are of poorer quality and could be rated as below standard.

Preschool facilities in Bahrain are divided into two types. The first one is nursery schools, for children under 3: there are only 8 nurseries with nearly 18 infants and toddlers in each group. The children's ages vary from 2 months to 3 years. The small number of facilities reflects a lack of interest in such service on the part of parents. It also suggests that the majority of working mothers with children under 3 years of age depend on other types of care; they either hire help to care for one or more children while the mother works, or they depend on their extended family, mostly the grandmother, to care for their children. But the main factor that discourages working mothers from seeking day-care nurseries as substitute care is the cost. Mothers pay nurseries an equivalent of $70 per month plus paying for milk and diapers. However, hiring foreign help, to take care of one or more children while the mother works, is less costly. Duties could also include housework, and this would considerably relieve the working mother. Another factor that makes such day-care services unappealing to the mothers is the low quality of the care and the standard of services they offer. Individual unlicensed home care also exists, but little is known about these facilities.

The second type is the kindergartens, for children from three- to 6-years old. Their programs tend to be subdivided along age lines and stress cognitive development and preparation for formal schooling and social development. Kindergartens have long waiting lists; this means that parents find such educational institutions very useful, in spite of being costly.

Goals, Objectives and Criteria of Child Care

There are three interrelated goals for child care, which sometimes conflict with each other: goals for parents, for children and for society.[15]

(a) Goals for parents: day-care programs in general have been mainly founded to satisfy the needs of adults rather than the needs of children. Parents have few options in terms of work schedules; however, working parents do want to promote optimal development in their children.
(b) Goals for children: day-care programs are seen as a means to promote the maximum development of a country's future citizens; programs are also seen as a way to compensate for overcrowded housing and as a source of enjoyment for children.
(c) Goals for society: day care can be seen as an instrument through which a society reaches many of its immediate and long-term goals and as a vehicle of social change. Furthermore, it facilitates the entry of young mothers into the labor force.

Out of these goals mentioned above, a comprehensive plan to meet the needs for more child-care services should be developed. The plan includes the following general objectives:

(a) Provide more day care services, sufficient to meet the

projected demands for the coming decade.

(b) Direct different government ministries to identify the needs of female employees who have preschool children under 6 years of age to establish day-care facilities and kindergartens close to their place of work.

(c) Support the efforts of women's associations as well as the efforts of the public and private sectors to expand current day care services.

(d) Encourage government subsidy for all preschool institutions.

(e) Improve the standard and quality of existing day-care services.

(f) Provide a stable, secure environment for the children attending day care.

Day-care objectives, however, differ slightly from kindergarten objectives in the sense that they focus mainly on the care for children whose mothers work. Kindergartens, on the other hand, include the previous objectives in addition to preparing children for formal education and providing them with the basic skills they need when they go to school.

As for criteria, quantitative as well as qualitative measures should be used in determining the effectiveness of the programs. Such measures include the cleanliness and nutritional adequacy, safety, health services, and an appropriate adult–child ratio. The qualitative measures are rather difficult to assess. They include cognitive, social and emotional development, especially for children under 3 years of age.

The staff training level is an important issue. Most of those who work in day-care facilities in Bahrain do not have any special training in childhood development. A 3-year training program after high school for a fully qualified teacher is required.

There is also a need for an increase in staffing, especially in facilities for young children; safety standards; space requirements providing for rest and nutrition; competency standards for care-givers; admission procedures; parental involvement; and a limited number of children per care giver in any family day care setting.

Alternatives

The number of day-care facilities in Bahrain has increased very rapidly in the last few years and has kept increasing until it has reached 64 units accommodating more than 5,000 preschool children in 1986. As mentioned earlier, many young children, especially those aged 3–6 years, are on the waiting lists of existing facilities. This shows clearly that the demand for spaces far exceeds supply, a problem that needs an urgent solution.

The nature of preschool care varies widely, from informal arrangements with a neighbor to licensed public or private day-care centers, nursery schools and kindergartens. The quality also varies, but the direction is towards more preschool services. The issue is no longer whether younger children will be enrolled in such programs, but how it will be done. Provision of day-care services could be implemented through the following organizations and alternatives:

1. Ministries and large companies.
2. Educational authorities.
3. Cooperatives: home care.
4. Child-care centers run by women's associations and supported by the government.
5. Subsidies for existing day-care facilities and the encouragement of licensed family day-care.
6. Adding-on a child development component to the existing facilities.

However, before presenting the above alternatives in more detail, we should look back to day-care services in the developed countries. Whereas developing countries are still in search for policy choices to solve the problem of young working mothers, we find that industrial countries have established many options regarding care for the very young whose parents work.

In a sense, Bahrain is fortunate in entering the child-care field late because there are many policy options that have been under experimentation for a long time in industrial countries. It is important to try to understand how certain countries have come to have certain policies in the child-care field. This will help us to understand the needs of our country for programs regarding child care.

It is more practical for developing countries to borrow or adapt specific ideas and policies that fit the needs of our societies. In addition, the examination of other systems may enable us to assess the impact of various approaches on families, on children and on the society as a whole, so that planning for child-care services would have the chance to be more workable and better implemented, bearing in mind the difference in culture and the level of development.

Each of the solutions reached by industrial countries has been formulated to meet the unique needs and goals of that country. However, the ways of dealing with child-care problems in all countries are continually changing in response to changing needs and conditions, which make it even more difficult to choose the best solution.

There are many alternatives in child-care programs in the industrialized countries; only three will be under discussion here:

(a) Day-care centers: (Krippen, crèche, day nurseries, preschool programs) for children under 3 years of age.
(b) Family day care (child minders) for children under 3 years of age.
(c) Kindergartens for children from 3–6 years of age.

The care and education of younger children in the industrialized countries were studied by many. However, I will limit my discussion here on one major study conducted by Kamerman and Kahn (1981). The authors reviewed and explored different alternatives for facilitating, supporting or providing out-of-home care for preschool children under 3 years of age. Such alternatives are intended to encourage labor market participation by parents without doing damage to children. Their study covers six industrial countries: France, the Federal Republic of Germany (FRG), German Democratic Republic (GDR), Hungary, Sweden and the United States (US). The effects, requirements, costs and optimal patterns of operation of centers and family day-care are discussed by the authors with great emphasis on the fact that day-care programs for children under three exist and are growing.[16]

The authors note that East European coverage clearly features centers. Although grandmothers and relatives still work as substitutes for working mothers, formal family day-care is no longer preferable. In Western Europe and in the United States, family day-care offers more coverage than center care. Arrangements for such care will be summarized in the following paragraphs.[17]

(a) The GDR embarked on a successful effort to improve the center care (Krippe) for young children. Krippen is an established, permanent institution. When housing blocks are constructed, facilities for kindergartens and elementary schools are automatically included in the planning, but the new innovative step was to include further day-care centers for children under 3 years of age. Currently, the joint construction of Krippen-Kindergarten is favored. The role of Krippen is perceived to be a help to parents in education and in health care when the mother works.

(b) In France, there are three main types of child care. The first type is the Ecole Maternelle, which enrolls all the 3–5 year olds. It is free and universal. Even children of 2–3 years of age of mothers who do not work have access if there is a place. The second type is the crèche, which serves those under three whose mothers work. The crèche is open to children aged 2½ months to 3 years. It operates on a 12-hour day, 5-days a week. In 1975, nearly 17% of the crèche were located in hospitals, public institutions and private firms. There are also a small number of mini-crèches, an experimental form in which a group of 12 children are cared for in private houses, staffed by publicly employed personnel. The third type is the family day-care: 1. the private nourice, 'child minder', or the family day-care mother (a women who cares for the children of others in her own home and who is paid by the child's parents). There were more unlicensed than licensed nourices in 1975 and 2. The crèche familiale, which is known elsewhere as a municipal family day-care that is publicly subsidized.

(c) Hungary's formal provision, like that of the GDR, is center care. Hungary provides strong financial support for at-home care by parents on leave from work for the first 3 years of a child's life. The support then ends but preschool provision is becoming universal: nearly 78% of the 3–5 cohort attended preschool. However, Hungary will now experiment with permitting mothers at home on child-care leave to take care of others' children, thus freeing more women to work if they wish to.

(d) Sweden has more private family day-care than center care, although center care for infants and toddlers is expected to increase. There is also more stress on quality. Both the physical environment and the curricula are carefully dealt with, and the standards are even higher than those of the other European countries. Sweden has made rapid progress in under-3 coverage while concentrating on the need for preschool space for its 3–6 year group. The government does not charge the full cost of care, but it subsidizes a substantial portion of the capital costs of group facilities. However, there are no commercial child care centers in Sweden.

(e) In the United States, the provision of day-care services is a result of the combined social and economic market. In 1975, a survey showed 7% of children under 3 were placed in non-relative family day care and 4% in group care (center care). In 1976, 49% of the 9.7 million children aged 3–5 years attended private nurseries or public and private kindergarten classes. The US places its public day-care in a social welfare context.

(f) The FRG has no distinct family policy. Like the US, the FRG relies heavily on unlicensed family day-care and has no clear policy of favoring a specific increase of care facilities for children under 3.

Kindergartens in most European countries for 3–6 year olds, fall under the Ministry of Education. They emphasize cognitive and social development and some do not charge a fee. The preschools are basically educational, with classes in both the morning and the afternoon. In the United States, kindergarten programs for 5-year-olds had been growing under the auspices of public schools, although numerous private programs existed. In 1974 more than 45% of the total population of 3 to 5-year-olds in the US was attending some sort of organized pre-primary program, compared with about 25% 10 years before. Kindergarten had become very much a public enterprise, with five out of six kindergarten children in public programs.[18]

After this presentation of different approaches and types of day care services in the industrialized countries, we will examine thoroughly the alternatives which would be suitable to Bahrain:

ALTERNATIVE 1 (MINISTRIES AND LARGE COMPANIES)

Working women formed 32% of the 24,583 government employees in 1984 (see Table 4.3). Most females are concentrated mainly in the Ministries of Health, Education and Labor and Social Affairs. Nearly 3,784 females (51%) work at the Ministry of Education, 2,537 females (49%) are employed at the Ministry of Health, and 238 females (49%) are employed at the Ministry of Labor and Social Affairs.

The number of working women with children under 6 years of age is not available except for the Ministry of Labor and Social Affairs. Its statistics show that mothers with preschool children

Table 4.3 *Staff in ministries of the state by sex, 1984*

Particulars	Male	Female	Total
Finance and National Economy	1,867	221	2,088
Commerce and Agriculture	683	64	747
Development and Industry	532	39	571
Education	3,767	3,784	7,551
Foreign Affairs	146	30	176
Health	2,688	2,537	5,225
Housing	395	121	516
Information	554	254	808
Justice and Islamic Affairs	403	10	413
Labor and Social Affairs	170	223	393
State for Cabinet Affairs	356	120	476
State for Legal Affairs	21	11	32
Work, Power and Water	3,952	301	4,253
High Council for Youth and Sports	143	41	184
Total	16,770	7,813	24,583

Sources: Statistical Abstracts 1984, op. cit., derived from Table 4.10, p. 170.

(from 1 month to 6 years) count for nearly 100 in 1986. In order to provide care for their infants, toddlers and preschool children, it is suggested that an integrated nursery–kindergarten facility suitable for such a population of different age variation be provided. Such a day-care center needs to be established near the mother's place of work, as this will keep mothers in better contact with their children and will allow them to breast feed the babies as well. This proximity may be a distinct advantage for nursing infants and for older children as well. Some critics are suggesting that once an infant has started to experience separation anxiety, frequent daily visits by the mother may be more painful than anything else. It is painful for the young child to know that the parent is nearby but still inaccessible.[19] However, other parents do prefer to have infants close by; this makes them feel more secure knowing if anything should happen, the parent could be there immediately.

In addition, work related day care is more likely to be adapted to a parent's unusual work schedule than is a neighborhood center. For example, a hospital day-care center might arrange its schedule around hospital worker's shifts.

Some critics of such an arrangement suggest that a possible disadvantage is the distance from home to center, especially if the distance is far and if the parents have to use public transportation. As for Bahrain, the distance from home to center is not an obstacle. The small size of Bahrain and the excellent network of roads and highways constructed recently have made it easier for parents to reach the areas farthest away in less than a 30-minute drive. Moreover, most working women drive their own cars and rarely use public transportation.

A similar program which was underway, was supposed to be established in 1979 by the Ministry of Health for children of working mothers at Sulmania Medical Center. The proposed day-care center was supposed to be a combination of play and learning. It was estimated that 12 babies and 40 toddlers could be accommodated in the center. The children once out of infancy, it was suggested, might join a family group and grow up in the same environment and with the same supervisor up to age 4. Those aged 4–6 years would have a separate group with an emphasis placed on education in their daily programs. The service would be available for two shifts, covering the hours from 6.15 am to 10.45 pm. The Ministry of Health proposed to provide the facilities and the trained staff, but the recurrent cost would be shared by the Ministry of Health together with mothers of the children using the facility.

The proposed program faced many obstacles that delayed implementation for a long period of time; finally, the program met a dead-end and was canceled. Various groups among the staff contributed to the failure of the program. Facing financial difficulty, the administration asked the mothers to pay a high fee ($80 per month). This offer was rejected by the mothers who asked for a lower fee. They preferred to bring in a foreign maid, who would take care of the child in addition to performing house work. In sum, one can say that many factors caused the program to fail. One factor was the high fee charged by the Health Authorities. Another factor was the unwillingness of the Health Ministry to take the program seriously and to provide financial support. The third factor could be the working mothers themselves; they did not make a greater effort and take a stand to force the health authorities to take them seriously.

Large companies such as Bahrain Petroleum Company (BAPCO), Aluminium Bahrain (ALBA), Arab Shipbuilding and Repair Yard (ASRY) and others that recruit many young mothers should take into consideration the needs of their female employees with children and start developing similar programs, bearing in mind that those semi-public companies do not pay any kind of taxes to the government.

Cost

The cost of each facility will differ according to the size of the population enrolled. The Ministry of Labor and Social Affairs, for example, with its small population of female workers (238 females) would have a smaller facility than the one that the Ministry of Education requires with its large number of female employees (2,537 females). It might require more than one day-care facility. The investment cost would be paid by the Ministry or the company concerned, whereas the recurrent cost would be shared by the parents of children enrolled in such facilities. However, people in Bahrain do not pay any kind of taxes to the government. Such arrangements for cost sharing would lighten the burden from employers.

Effectiveness

This alternative is highly feasible if it is planned carefully. Government ministries with a large percentage of working females should take the initiative and start such programs; this in turn, will make it easier for other large companies to follow suit.

ALTERNATIVE 2 (EDUCATIONAL AUTHORITIES)

Recent development in child-care indicates that the age at which children start formal schooling is dropping. In many developed countries, kindergarten for 5 year olds has become a necessity.

This development suggests that the Ministry of Education, already responsible for the education of children 3–6 years old, should take an initiative to eliminate the shortage in child-care facilities – becuase of the high cost for such a program, the Ministry of Education could begin by adding classes to the existing elementary schools. The first stage of this program would be limited to the 5-year-olds in Bahrain. There is no exact figure on the number of children of that age. However, the population aged 5–9 years in 1986 is expected to reach 45,188.[20] This means that the number of 5-year-old children could be estimated to range from 9,000 to 10,000 children. Nearly 300 classrooms woud then need to be built and equipped in different elementary schools; in addition, 600 trained teachers would need to be recruited for the program. The number of public elementary schools in Bahrain reached 102 for both sexes in 1986. This means that the program need to be completed in 3 years time to reduce the financial burden on the budget. Each year one class would be started in each elementary school. By the end of the third year, the entire population of 5-year-olds would be enrolled in the school system.

Cost

The most serious problem facing this program is the high cost of constructing the large number of new classrooms, besides training and recruiting the personnel.

The investment cost which includes the construction of nearly 300 new classrooms, the purchase of equipment and audiovisual aids, and the training of 600 staff, would cost nearly $15 m. The recurrent cost, on the other hand, which would include staff salaries, would cost $5 m annually. Parents would share the cost with the government and pay a monthly fee. This would reduce the recurrent cost to a great extent.

Effectiveness

This alternative would help the majority of children under 6 years of age to receive an education at a reasonable cost. In addition, it would shift nearly half of the recurrent cost from the government to the parents.

ALTERNATIVE 3 (COOPERATIVES: HOME CARE)

Cooperative child-care is usually established by a group of working mothers in the home of one of the group members, either because of the lack of such facilities in their own neighborhood or, in some cases, because of their concern about interference by the government in family matters. But whereas parent cooperatives often represent a solution to the participation goal, they are hardly the answer for child care in most places. Working parents cannot participate adequately. The cooperative mode depends on the continued support of all group members. It is difficult to decide wether cooperative child-care centers would be successful in a place like Bahrain, where many women are illiterate and lack the basic awareness to take the initiative of forming a cooperative.

Cost

It is expected that such arrangement would cost little compared to other arrangements, especially in relation to the building construction and staff salaries.

Effectiveness

This alternative is not feasible. It does not meet the criteria of cleanliness and proper supervision.

ALTERNATIVE 4: (CHILD-CARE CENTERS RUN BY WOMEN'S ASSOCIATIONS AND SUPPORTED BY THE GOVERNMENT)

Day-care nurseries and kindergartens under the auspices of women's associations are considered to have a high quality of services. Quantity is more of a problem in such day care. What is needed is further construction of day-care centers by the government, because this form of care has proved to be more popular and more accepted in different places of the world.

Cost

Women's associations could raise funding for this purpose through different ways and means and could participate with the government in the construction of the buildings. Parents, in addition, would pay a small monthly fee.

Effectiveness

This alternative is highly feasible if it is planned carefully. Nurseries and kindergartens run by women's associations have proved to be more efficient than those run by private individuals. And women's associations could continue to run them if they had the financial support of the government.

ALTERNATIVE 5 (SUBSIDIES FOR EXISTING DAY-CARE FACILITIES AND ENCOURGEMENT OF LICENSED FAMILY DAY-CARE)

As mentioned earlier, existing day-care facilities of all kinds are spreading very rapidly; this reflects the great demand for such services. The main obstacles that keep existing facilities from improving the quality and standards of services is the lack of funds. Increasing the tuition fees would not solve the problem; on the contrary, it would discourage parents with limited income from enrolling their children in day-care facilities. The government subsidizes all day-care nurseries and kindergartens run by women's associations in Bahrain, whereas those run by private individuals are left without any kind of assistance; this makes their services deteriorate in the long run.

One solution is for the government to subsidize the private

day-care nurseries and kindergartens to lighten the cost burden from schools and parents as well. At the same time, financial assistance granted to the facilities run by women's associations needs to be raised.

One important institution that needs more attention is the family day-care nursery, both licensed and unlicensed. Unlicensed family day-care does exist in Bahrain, and it is considered to offer a preferable arrangement. Family day-care, simply because it takes place in homes, may not necessarily provide safety: for example, electrical outlets may be uncovered, medicines may be within easy reach of children and there may be little open space for activities. The government should check on such unlicensed facilities in order to ensure a safe and healthy environment for young children.

Cost

This alternative would be reasonable in cost because the facilities already exist.

Effectiveness

The government subsidy of family day-care would be feasible as this would enhance the quality and adequacy of the day-care facility.

ALTERNATIVE 6 (ADDING-ON A CHILD DEVELOPMENT COMPONENT TO THE EXISTING FACILITIES)

Centers that were established for a different purpose other than child care could be used as child-care facilities. Adding-on a child development component to other services delivered in existing centers created for other purposes has many advantages. The cost might be low because much of the physical and organizational infrastructure already exists. Furthermore, it could be an easy way of integrating components because the structure and staff for program responsibility will already have been established.[21]

The following existing facilities would be suitable ones for adding-on programs:

1. *Health centers* (For children 0–3 years-old)
   There are 17 health centers distributed in different urban and rural areas in Bahrain.[22] Most were built in recent years and have spacious, modern buildings surrounded by large gardens. Health centers offer free treatment, as do all health services in Bahrain.

   Providing or adding one spacious room within the center to be used as a day-care nursery for young infants and toddlers is a practical idea. The nursery could make use of the doctors and nurses who work in the health center. They could treat sick children or advise the staff on health matters.

   The Ministry of Labor and Social Affairs would supply the facility with equipment and furniture and the Ministry of Education would provide the trained staff, which would not have to exceed more the 2 per center because all the other services already exist. Each center could easily accommodate 10–12 children under 3 years of age; this means that all the 17 centers would serve nearly 200 infants and toddlers of working mothers. A small fee could be charged to parents in order to help towards the cost of milk, nappies and other necessary items.
2. *Social Centers* (For children 0–3-years-old)
   Social centers in Bahrain were established more recently to serve local communities in different areas, particularly in the field of child and mother welfare. They are also used as training centers for women to learn such skills as sewing and handicrafts. All the centers are spacious and surrounded by large gardens. In each center, there is a kindergarten for children aged 3–6-years-old. This is in the garden and near the social center. There are five such kindergartens, all run by women's associations.

   It is suggested that one spacious room, for example a large auditorium, often not in use, could be converted into a day-care nursery to accommodate 20 infants and toddlers of working mothers. A small fee would be charged parents to cover part of the expense. The five centers could easily accommodate more than 100 children under 3 years of age.
3. *Women's and other cultural and professional associations, and sports clubs* (For children age 0–3-years-old)

All women's associations in Bahrain are already involved in child care. Many are situated in modest buildings not suitable for child-care use. However, a spacious room could be built onto the main building to be used as a nursery for 10 infants and toddlers.

Sports clubs could be used for this purpose as well, especially those that have recently accepted young women as members. Sports clubs are attended by members in the afternoons, so that in the morning they are usually closed. For this reason, some sports clubs could be used in the morning as child-care facilities to serve children under 3 years of age. This alternative would accommodate nearly 100 children under 3 years of age.

Cost

The cost would be moderately low because all the facilities are already in place. The parents would be charged a small fee.

Effectiveness

This alternative would be highly feasible if planned carefully.

Conclusion

There are three important administrative and financial issues that need to be put into effect before any of the program is implemented: (a) integration of all child-care services through a coordinative committee or a high council for child welfare and development; (b) staff training and; (c) funding of the programs.

COORDINATIVE COMMITTEE

As mentioned earlier, child-care services in Bahrain suffer from conflicting administrative roles. Three governmental bodies (the Ministries of Education, Labor and Social Affairs, and the High Council for Youth and Sports) are assigned to plan and execute child care services, each one on its own, without consultation with each other. The Ministry of Health is left with no role in supervising or planning services. this fragmentation weakens child-care services and makes coordination nearly impossible among the four government departments. Therefore, it is suggested that all child-care programs be integrated in their planning and administration so that parents can learn about and participate in programs operating in various systems, public and private. A coordinative committee should be formed to include all four governmental bodies dealing with child care as well as representatives of the five women's associations. The committee would meet periodically to assess and evaluate different child-care programs and recommend steps in future planning.

STAFF TRAINING

Lack of trained staff is a major constraint on expanding child-care provisions. As a result of this shortage, many working mothers have been obliged to leave their preschool children in existing day-care facilities, ones that fail to meet adequately the young child's needs for emotional care and intellectual stimulation. To solve this problem requires both a new orientation of the staff and an improvement in adult/child ratio.

The staff are considered the most important part of the entire preschool system. The day-care staff members in Bahrain do not have special college training for day-care work, especially in the field of childhood development. They are typically educated females who have had either elementary or some high school education. The number of teachers working without any special training is probably very high. In addition, those who were not accepted as teachers in public schools turn back to preschool teaching and accept the extremely low pay offered by preschools in general. Besides the low salaries, preschool employees are not allowed to be covered under the social insurance operated by the government; this makes them feel more financially insecure.

Staff training, however, has been taken more seriously in recent years. Many training sessions have taken place since 1981. The Ministry of Labor and Social Affairs and the High Council for Youth and Sports, with the help of the UNICEF, had held many training sessions for child care personnel and administrators. In 1983, the Ministry of Education took responsibility for the training. Such training programs have proved to have little effect in raising the standard and quality of the staff.

Preschool teachers need to be trained more extensively. They should be offered a 2- to 3-year program at Bahrain University, where similar programs are offered for elementary teachers. Training needs to focus on important subjects in the fields of child psychology, children's literature, the hygiene of preschoolers and other important topics regarding child education. The proposed 2- to 3-year program for training should follow high school; it is assumed that a general education has already been accomplished, so that the years of training for preschool teaching are devoted entirely to professional learning.

COST

The government role in the provision of child care can be direct, by financing construction and paying the operating costs of child-care centers and nurseries; or it can be indirect, by subsidizing child-care programs, supervising and monitoring standards through requiring the licensing of private child-care arrangements. Women's associations, with the cooperation of parents, could play a major role in contributing to the cost of child-care programs, through different means of fund raising.

The provision of proper child-care arrangements that would satisfy all groups is rather difficult to develop. For parents who, out of necessity or preference, choose some form of substitute care, six alternatives were presented including different kinds of settings for different age groups. Such arrangements would meet the immediate needs for more child-care programs. Each of the six alternatives meets part of the criteria in terms of cost, adequacy, cleanliness, trained staff and low adult–child ratio.

The first alternative suggests that government ministries and companies with a large population of working mothers of young children provide day-care centers for those children. This alternative is highly feasible if the parents manage to pay a small amount of the total cost, in other words, if they pay less money than what they already pay for a foreign maid. Children under 3 years of age would benefit most from this setting.

The second alternative proposes that the Ministry of Education should add classes to the existing elementary schools for children 5 years of age. These account for nearly 10,000 of the entire population. This alternative would have little chance to be implemented because of its high cost.

The third alternative deals with cooperative child care and

seems the least feasible of all. The inability of working mothers in Bahrain to organize in order to form cooperatives is one major factor. The cost would be low, but other criteria such as adequacy and efficiency would be lacking.

The fourth alternative calls for support by the government of women's associations in their effort to establish more child-care centers. This opinion would have a greater chance of success, because such arrangements already exist. These programs have also proved to be more popular and efficient than the rest of the day-care programs. This alternative is considered highly feasible.

The fifth alternative urges the government to subsidize existing day-care facilities so that they can become more efficient and serve more children. The alternative is considered highly effective because it would not cost much; at the same time, it would improve the quality of existing day care.

The last alternative (adding-on to existing facilities) is the most feasible of all the alternatives for children under 3 years of age. The cost would be low as most of the facilities and staff have already been established.

The following exhibit will present a summary of the effectiveness and cost of the various alternatives for the initial year.

Different alternatives	No. of children served	Cost	Adequacy & efficiency	Effectiveness
Alternative one (short & long term) (0–6 yrs)	not known	not known	+	High
Alternative two (long term) (5 yrs)	10,000	$20 million	+	Moderate
Alternative three (long term) (0–3 yrs)	not known	not known	–	Low

(continued)

Different alternatives	No. of children served	Cost	Adequacy & efficiency	Effectiveness
Alternative four (short & long term) (0–6 yrs)	not known	not known	+	High
Alternative five (long term) (0–6 yrs)	5,000	not known	+	High
Alternative six (short term) (0–3 yrs)	400	not known	+	High

Therefore, to meet the demands for more child-care services, alternative 5 is recommended for the long-term basis; alternatives 1, 4 and 6 are recommended for short- and long-term basis; and alternative 3 is not recommended at present.

Notes

1. Sheila B. Kamerman and Alfred J. Kahn (Eds), *Family Policy; Government and Families in Fourteen Countries*, New York: Columbia University Press, 1978, p. 484.
2. *A Survey on Women in the Labor Force in Bahrain*, Ministry of Labor and Social Affairs, 1980. (Arabic)
3. Sheila Kamerman and Alfred Kahn, *Child Care, Family Benefits, and Working Parents*, New York: Columbia University Press, 1981, p. 249.
4. Mia Kellmer and Sadhya Naidoo, *Early Child Care in Britain*, London: Gordon and Breach, 1975, p. 23.
5. *Towards a National Policy for Children and Families*, Washington, D.C: National Academy of Sciences, 1976, p. 7.
6. Sheila Kamerman and Alfred Kahn, *Child Care, Family Benefits, and Working Parents*, New York: Columbia University Press, 1981, p. 128.
7. Jay Belsky and Laurence Steinberg, 'The Effects of Day Care: a Critical Review', *Child Development*, vol. 49 (1978) pp. 929–49.

8. K. Alison Clarke-Stewart & Greta G. Fein, 'Early Childhool Programs', in M. M. Maith & J. J. Campos (eds), P. H. Mussen (Series Ed.) *Handbook of Child Psychology: Vol. 2, Infancy & Developmental Psychology* John Wiley: New York.
9. *Towards a National Policy for Children and Families*, Washington D.C., National Academy of Sciences, 1976, p. 71.
10. Jay Belsky, 'Infant Care: A Case for Concern?', *Bulletin of The National Center for Clinical Infant Programs*, vol. VI, no. 5 (Sept. 1986) p. 4.
11. Mamdooh Al-Mubayedh and Baheya Al-Jishi, *Taqweem Awdha' Door Al-Hadhana wa Reyadh Al-Atfal Al-wataneya fil-Bahrain, dirasah mydaneya* (Assessing child care services in Bahrain: a field study), The High Council for Youth and Sports and the UNICEF, 1980, p. 62. (Arabic).
12. *Statistical Abstract/1984*, Council of Ministers, Central Statistics Organization, Bahrain, Dec. 1985, Table 2.26, p. 47.
13. *Social Indicators for Bahrain*, Ministry of Labor and Social Affairs, Bahrain (Dec. 1982) Table 7-14, p. 94.
14. Mamdooh Almubayedh and Baheya Al-Jishi, *Teqweem Awdha' Door Al-Hadhana wa Reyadh Al-Atfal Al-wataneya fil Bahrain, dirasa mydaneya*, (Assessing child care services in Bahrain: a field study), the High Council for Youth and Sports, and the UNICEF, 1980, p. 64. (Arabic.)
15. Nancy M. Robinson, Halbert B. Robinson, Martha Darling and Gretchen Holm, *A World of Children: Day Care and Preschool Institutions*, Monterey, Calif.: Brooks/Cole Publishing Co., 1979, pp. 92–110.
16. Sheila Kamerman and Alfred Kahn, *Child Care, Family Benefits, and Working Parents*, New York: Columbia University Press, 1981, p. 197.
17. Ibid., pp. 119–202.
18. Nancy Robinson, Halbert B. Robinson, Mark Darling and Gretch Hold, *A World of Children: Day Care and Preschool Institutions*, Monterey, Calif.: Brooks/Cole Publishing Co., 1979, pp. 30–2.
19. Peggy Daly Pizzo, *The Infant Day Care Debate: Not Whether But How*, Day Care and Child Development Council of America, Washington, D.C., p. 12.
20. *Statistical Abstracts/1984*, Council of Ministers, Central Statistics Organization, Bahrain (Dec. 1985) Table 2.26, p. 47.
21. Robert G. Myers, *Programming for Early Childhood Care and Development, Complementary Approaches and Program Option*, Chapter V, produced for UNICEF field manual, 1986, p. 14.
22. *Statistical Abstracts/1984*, Council of ministers, Central Statistics Organization, Bahrain (Dec. 1985) Table 6.01, p. 172.

Chapter Five

Education and Female Employment

People are not made literate; they make themselves literate.[1]

Bahrain founded public education in 1919, earlier than any other Gulf state. But the first girls' primary school was established earlier in 1892 by the American Arabian Mission. Between 1931 and 1983, investment in public education increased dramatically. The number of students enrolled in schools increased from 500 boys and 100 girls in 1931, to 1,750 boys and 1,288 girls in 1946; 4,500 boys and 2,300 girls in 1953, to 30,202 boys and 23,459 girls in 1974; this was about a quarter of the total population of Bahrain at that time. The number kept rising until it reached a total of 78,797 (41,477 boys and 37,320 girls) aged 6–21 years in 1983–84.[2] This figure does not include students who were enrolled in private schools where their number reached 4,291 males and 4,056 females for the same year.

Like other developing countries, Bahrain is a nation of young people. The 1971 census reveals that nearly 59.6% of the population was under 20 years of age. This high percentage of growth in the population is also reflected in the 1981 census. Nearly 54.4% of Bahrain's population was under 20 years of age. The population is expected to double within a generation's time. This substantial increase of youth under 20 years of age adds greatly to the amount of strain under which the educational system functions.

But despite the increase in school enrollment for both sexes, nearly half the school-age population (42,614) between 5–24 years of age did not attend school in 1971, whereas in 1981 only 20% of school-age population between 5–19 years of age did not attend school. This is still a high percentage, which indicates that the educational system failed to reach a large number of the population, especially females, who account for 80% of all the

Table 5.1 *Non-school attending population 5–24 years of age by single years of age and sex (Bahraini nationals), 1971*

Age	Males	Females	Total
5	3,113	3,033	6,146
6	2,330	2,399	4,729
7	1,143	1,408	2,551
8	546	1,053	1,599
9	243	919	1,162
10	276	955	1,231
11	148	663	811
12	257	1,011	1,268
13	183	712	895
14	314	1,058	1,372
15	428	948	1,376
16	611	1,123	1,734
17	708	983	1,691
18	1,320	1,737	3,057
19	1,026	964	1,990
20	1,790	2,102	3,892
21	850	669	1,519
22	1,276	1,246	2,522
23	885	665	1,550
24	777	742	1,519
Total	18,224	24,390	42,614

Sources: Nakleh, Emile, op. cit., derived from Table 2-7, p. 22.

illiterate population aged 10–44 years in Bahrain.

Many factors could be related to such a low percentage of student enrollment, but the lack of legislation for compulsory education is considered to be a major factor. The voluntary nature of education has been a mixed blessing: on the one hand, the pressure on the schools was not very high, but, on the other hand, the rate of illiteracy has increased, especially within the female school-age population.[3] Parents, especially those in rural areas, are reluctant to send their daughters to school. As Table 5.1 indicates, because education is not compulsory, a large number of school-age girls are kept out of school. In the 8–16 age group, three to four times as many girls as boys do not attend school.

Furthermore, the educational system in Bahrain is not well-adapted to the needs of modern economic development. Despite the rapid increase in the educational attainments of graduates from the education and training systems, available national manpower in the Gulf states, including Bahrain, will not fulfill the requirements, especially at the professional and technical level. In Bahrain, for example, the number of secondary students enrolled in the year 1983/84 reached 12,799, whereas those enrolled in different colleges in Bahrain and abroad reached 3,309 students for the same year. These figures fall short of meeting labor market demands in a place where foreigners constitute nearly 60% of the labor force. The World Bank study predicts that the reliance on non-nationals in the Gulf state cannot be changed significantly in the short and medium term by current educational policies and training programs.[4]

However, a closer examination of the educational system indicates a dualism in the system as a whole. The task facing the educators in Bahrain and in the rest of the Gulf states, namely, to produce a modern, mainly Western-motivated, industrial work-force, filled with a sense of traditional Moslem values – is a discouraging one. Birks and Rimmer explain the difference in the philosophies of education in the Gulf region and the West. The educational systems in the West win popular approval by avoiding indoctrination, and the students who learn to reason, win praise and promotion. Their merit is recognized and a technological society makes way for their climb to positions of power. Such a philosophy contradicts the attitudes in the Gulf states where Islamic teachings live and science must accommodate itself to it. In addition, educational systems win popular approval by their affirmation of religion, and well-educated people are believed to be those who have learned the word of God. Students who prove their ability to memorize revealed truth correctly, and who can quote it in appropriate contexts, win praise and respect today as in the past. Such students are encouraged by society.[5] Furthermore, schools are required to foster belief in Islam. At the same time they are required to prepare students for life in a modern, technological society, where students will work after graduation. Such conflict is escalated when educational authorities in the Gulf region call upon the services of educationalists from other Arab states or upon educationalists from the West. Arab advisers reflect the cultural values of a society in which the conflict between Islam, technology and modern political ideologies is not yet resolved. Educationalists from the West are bound by different values, which are in conflict with many Islamic teachings: one such value is that man is master of his own fate. Therefore, when Western educationalists propose such things to devise curricula designed to turn him into a Western-type thinker, they arouse suspicion and hostility. Thus, the clash between modern economic development and traditional Islamic values enters the heart of the process of education.[6]

Another problem of great importance is the conflict between educational planners and economic planners. Educationalists see education as providing a means of personal development and mental enrichment for the student, and thus, the stress of this system is upon the liberal arts. Economic planners, on the other hand, see the purpose of the developing education systems as a service to the economy, and as a means of preparing qualified and motivated workers, nationals who will replace non-national workers who already dominate the modern sectors of the economy.[7]

EDUCATION AND FEMALE EMPLOYMENT

Education has a great influence on changing the situation of women. The relationship between female education and employment has been studied and discussed by many (Youssef, 1977; Al-Kazi, 1985; Massialas and Mikati, 1985). Those studies demonstrated a close relationship between the increased rates of women's participation in the labor force and their access to education: the higher the level of education, the greater the women's employability. Youssef (1977) discusses the impact of education on women's employability in different Moslem countries. She finds a strong correlation between the female literacy level and the access of women to the labor market: the higher the female illiteracy rates, the lower the women's access to non-agricultural employment and the lower the per capita GNP.[8]

In her assessment of the impact of education on women's economic participation in Kuwait, Al-Kazi (1985) observes that as Kuwaiti women made rapid progress in educational attainment, they similarly entered in greater numbers into the labor force. In 1970, only 2% of Kuwaiti women were in the labor force, whereas in 1980 the number increased to 10%. In the total Kuwaiti labor force, the percentage of Kuwaiti females increased from 3% in 1970 to 13% in 1980. Al-Kazi examines the census data (1980) for Kuwait and concludes that as the educational level for women rises, a greater proportion of them are economically active. In 1980, less than 1% of illiterate Kuwaiti women were employed, whereas 43% of those with secondary school certificates were employed. Among university graduates, nearly 82% of Kuwaiti were working: this supports the strong positive impact of education on economic participation.[9]

Massails and Mikati (1985) describe some trends in women's education in the Arab World regarding developments in education in the last 10 to 20 years. Although their data are not recent (going back to 1975), they identified some possible links between the education of Arab women and their participation in the labor force. In 1975, the ILO estimated the total number of females who joined the labor market in the Arab World to have reached only 9% of the total work force. This low percentage of female employability is below the rates for the developed, as well as for the developing world, which were over 40% and 26% of the working population respectively. The authors examine different statistics and studies that were conducted in many Arab countries and conclude by supporting the idea that as the educational level for women rises, a greater proportion of females join the labor force.[10]

Such findings could be applied to statistical data for employed females in Bahrain, who are 15 years and over. Table 5.2 shows the distribution of the employed Bahraini population at various educational levels. It shows also that illiteracy rates of females are much higher than those of males in the 1981 census. Table 5.2 also reveals that as the female educational level rises, a higher percentage of women join the labor force. Among the 7,874 employed Bahraini females, only 631 females (nearly 8% of the female working population) are illiterate. Those who can barely read and write or have acquired primary education constitute only 9%. Working females with a secondary education make up 42% of the population. (This is the largest group among the different educational levels.) And females who have acquired a diploma or a college degree or a higher degree constitute 32% of the total employed females.

Table 5.2 *Employed Bahraini populaton, 15-years and over, by sex, employment status, and highest level achieved 1981*

Sex and Employment Status	HIGHEST LEVEL ACHIEVED										
	Illiterate	Read and Write	Primary	Inter-mediate	Secondary	Diploma	BA or BSc	Master's Degree	PhD equivalent	Not Stated	Total
Male	13,528	10,339	6,990	5,719	8,366	2,439	1,668	214	36	5	49,304
Government and Semi-Government Employee	4,211	3,779	3,005	2,574	3,887	1,273	927	119	22	2	19,799
Employee of Private Company	3,873	3,521	2,690	2,206	3,288	834	440	54	3	2	16,911
Self-Employed	4,889	2,297	824	524	599	157	130	20	2	1	9,443
Employer	226	291	136	115	208	72	55	5	—	—	1,108
Paid Servant	72	35	4	5	1	—	—	—	—	—	117
Unpaid Worker	37	41	18	12	14	3	1	—	—	—	126
Not Stated	11	13	5	5	4	—	1	—	—	—	39
Not Applicable	209	362	308	278	365	100	114	16	9	—	1,761
Female	631	287	438	692	3,344	1,576	864	38	3	1	7,074
Government and Semi-Government Employee	486	192	307	444	1,928	1,239	699	32	3	1	5,331
Employee of Private Company	38	53	109	230	1,332	301	137	5	—	—	2,205
Self-Employed	44	15	5	5	24	8	4	1	—	—	106
Employer	2	2	7	—	5	3	3	—	—	—	22
Paid Servant	47	15	2	1	—	—	—	—	—	—	65
Unpaid Worker	6	2	—	—	3	—	—	—	—	—	11
Not Stated	2	—	—	1	6	—	—	—	—	—	9
Not applicable	6	8	8	11	46	25	21	—	—	—	125
Total	14,159	10,626	7,428	6,411	11,710	4,015	2,532	252	39	6	57,178

Government and Semi-Government Employee	4,697	3,971	3,312	3,018	5,815	2,512	1,626	151	25	3	25,130
Employee of Private Company	3,911	3,574	2,799	2,436	4,620	1,135	5[illegible]	59	3	2	19,116
Self-Employed	4,933	2,312	829	529	623	165	134	21	2	1	9,549
Employer	228	293	143	115	213	75	58	5	—	—	1,130
Paid Servant	119	50	6	6	1	—	—	—	—	—	182
Unpaid Worker	43	43	18	12	17	3	[illegible]	—	—	—	137
Not Stated	13	13	5	6	10	—	1	—	—	—	48
Not Applicable	215	370	316	289	411	125	135	16	9	—	1,886

Not Applicable (For Bahraini Population Abroad)

Sources: Bahrain Census of Population and Housing/1981, op. cit., derived from Table 398, p. 175

THE ILLITERACY PROBLEM IN BAHRAIN

The 1958 UNESCO General Conference recommended the following definition of the illiterate person: one who cannot with understanding both read and write a short, simple statement about his everyday life. In 1978, the General Conference added to this definition by adapting a revised definition: 'a person is functionally illiterate who cannot engage in all those activities in which literacy is required for effective functioning of his group and community and also for enabling him to continue to use reading, writing and calculation for his own community's development'.[11] However, the measure of functional literacy is not fixed; it is steadily being adjusted upward. The level of qualification that allowed a person to be employed in the recent past may not be sufficient in the future or even at present. Illiteracy among the female population in Bahrain is extremely high. Table 5.3 reveals a warning signal on illiteracy when the number of illiterate men and women aged 10 years and over has

Table 5.3 *Illiterate Bahraini population (10 years and over) by age and sex (1981 census)*

	Sex		
Age Group	Male	Female	Total
10–14	416	1,628	2,044
15–19	685	2,443	3,128
20–24	787	3,004	3,791
25–29	764	2,982	3,746
30–34	733	2,909	3,642
35–39	1,032	3,493	4,525
40–44	1,801	4,048	5,849
45–49	2,269	3,682	5,951
50–54	2,647	3,344	5,991
55–59	2,119	2,238	4,357
60–64	1,913	2,011	3,924
65 Years & Over	2,959	3,332	6,291
Total	18,125	35,114	53,239

Source: Statistical Abstracts 1983, op. cit., derived from Table 13, p. 27.

reached 53,239. Women form the majority, 35,114, or nearly 66% of the total.

The high percentage of illiterate females becomes even higher among those aged 10–44 years. Statistics show that illiterate persons aged 10–44 years totaled 26,724; 6,218 males and 20,506 females, which means that females constitute 80% of all illiterate persons aged 10–44 years. Such a high female illiteracy rate limits, to a great extent, the participation of women in the labor force.

In the private sector, the number of female workers increased from 1,435 in 1979 to 2,457 in 1982; an increase of 71.2% in 3 years only. Table 5.2 shows that the number of illiterate workers in the private sector reached 14,796 workers who represent 18.7% of a total of 78,983 workers. It shows also that the number of illiterate Bahraini female workers was only 71 out of a total of 3,460 or about 2% of the total female work force at all educational levels. The public sector also has a low percentage of illiterate female workers (Table 5.2); out of a total of 5,331 Bahraini female workers, there are only 486 illiterate female workers, about 9% of the total.

Such a low percentage of illiterate female workers in both public and private sectors indicates that illiterate female workers have little opportunity for joining the labor market; it also indicates that education plays an important role in integrating more females into the modern sector of the economy.

The Strategy of Planning a Literacy Program for Bahrain

The rate of illiteracy in a given community is believed to have an effect on people's attitudes and behaviour in regard to literacy training. Literacy training in a community where illiteracy is still widespread differs a great deal from the training needed for a community with less illiteracy. Furthermore, illiteracy rates of a given community provide valuable information for planners to decide which strategy to adopt for its eradication. Clerck considers four distinct milieux in regard to illiteracy:[12]

1. A pre-literate milieu, where oral communication is used most and life is lived as though writing and the printed word did not exist. The literacy rate in a milieu of this

type exceeds 75%. The author gives Chad as an example: illiteracy rates in some parts of Chad reach 83% for men and 99% for women. The program for teaching written arithmetic has been very successful for both men and women because it has been aimed at enabling peasants to market the cotton they produced. It has enabled them to check the weight and value of their crops and to create a self-managed market.

2. The predominantly illiterate milieu, which already includes a minority of literates. This type of milieu has an illiteracy rate between 50% to 75% of the adult population. A literacy program which helps in achieving socio-economic and political changes and enhances the development process has a good chance of succeeding if it is well conducted. Tanzania conducted such a program and succeeded in reducing illiteracy in its adult population from 67% in 1967 to 39% in 1976, and this has continued to decline reaching 10% at present.
3. A milieu, which is becoming literate, in which a majority of persons practice reading and writing for different purposes. The illiteracy rate in such a milieu varies between 25% to 50%. The majority of the illiterates is composed of women and the members of the older generation. Illiterates in such a milieu are ashamed to be so.
4. The literate milieu with an illiteracy rate of less than 25%, where it is normal to be able to read and write. Illiteracy in this case would be encountered only in small groups of people.

According to the above classification, Bahrain could be placed in the third milieu: one that is becoming literate – one in which 30% of the population 10 years of age and over is illiterate. The following statistics reveal how the illiteracy rates break down. Illiterates among women number as high as 80% of the total illiterates aged 10–44 years; and nearly half the illiterate population is made up of members of the older generation aged 45 years and over. Illiterate men aged 10–44 years form a small percentage (17.7%) of the total illiterate population.

Realizing that the problem of illiteracy in Bahrain is mainly a problem of illiteracy among women, one has to focus on women's programs that fulfill women's needs. Selective programs designed for a target population (women) are more suitable than a mass campaign for the initial phase.

However, in setting up a literacy program for women, planners should not isolate women from the general development programs. Literacy programs aim at integrating women fully into the development process in order to achieve equal rights in society. Because of the multiple roles played by women as housewives, mothers and/or working women, literacy programs should be related to such roles.

In evaluating India's experience in the women's literacy program, Dighe presents several issues that should be taken into consideration in the designing of women's literacy programs:[13]

1. Learner or women centered programs: approaches should be formulated from learner-centered priorities and objectives. The content of the educational program is designed after a long process of exploration and discussions. The program must be flexible in terms of content, time and location to serve different needs. Planner also should avoid focusing only on women but rather should emphasize the complementary responsibilities of men and women as partners in the development process. It should be borne in mind that there are certain areas that concern women more than men, and the educational program itself could begin by focusing on them.
2. Learning to improve earnings: the program should be designed in a way that enables illiterate women to learn ways to increase their incomes.
3. Mobilizing women toward participation in collective action and involvement in the decision-making process.

In addition to the above strategy, planners should put into consideration the two models that could be adapted in designing a literacy program: the top-down model, which starts with planning at the central level and goes down to planning at the community level, and the grass roots approach or bottom-up model, which starts with planning at the village level and goes up gradually to planning at the national level.[14] Those two models should be seen as complementary rather than as opposed to each other, because the main role of literacy and post-literacy planning is to bring together local needs and national development objectives.

Goals, Objectives and Criteria

Illiteracy imposes great constraints on adults; it also constitutes a major obstacle to the participation of large sections of society in development. As stated earlier, illiteracy is most widespread among the female population. Certain measures need to be undertaken when implementing a literacy program.

To achieve a successful literacy program in Bahrain, the following should be the goals:

1. To eradicate illiteracy among the entire population in Bahrain.
2. To establish adult education as an integral and permanent part of the educational system.

From these general goals, certain qualitative and quantitative objectives would be formulated:

(a) To improve literacy programs on different levels by categorizing illiterate males and females according to their ages; by transferring those under 10 years of age to regular public schools; by training teachers and increasing their salaries.
(b) To link the literacy campaign with vocational training, especially for workers capable of further study.
(c) To utilize the mass media as a major instrument for the elimination of illiteracy.

Although the previous objectives are suitable for the entire illiterate population of Bahrain, illiterate females would have some different objectives that are related to their concerns, their needs and their problems. Such objectives include the following:

(a) To help their children understand school assignments and homework.
(b) To learn ways to increase their income and to improve their living conditions in general.

(c) To become effective within their community.

The following criteria should be followed to insure an effective program.

(a) Training the staff; assessing the adequacy of the curriculum; applying modern tools and equipment in teaching and using different audiovisual aids.
(b) Keeping track of the number of women who join the literacy campaign each year.
(c) Asessing the program cost and ways to minimize them.

Current Literacy Programs in Bahrain

A literacy campaign was started in Bahrain in the early 1940s by a group of volunteers who opened a few literacy classes for 70 adult students. In the 1960s more classes were opened for males and females, and later, a committee was formed to evaluate and supervise literacy activities. The committee included members from different youth clubs and women's organizations.[15]

In 1971, the Ministry of Education took the responsibility for literacy education. At that period, the number of illiterate persons aged 10–44 years reached 41,345 persons: 12,987 males and 28,358 females. A year later, 30 classes were opened with a budget of 26,262 Bahraini Dinars, an amount equivalent to $60,000.

The number of females who joined literacy programs has increased over the years. In 1973–74, 576 males and 576 females were enrolled in the program. In 1974–75, the number of females increased to 1,732, nearly 60% of the total. In 1976/77, female enrollment reached 4,521 or 74.4% of the total whereas the percentage of males who joined literacy classes kept decreasing until it reached 21.6% in 1982/83. In other words, all literacy plans prior to the 5 year plan, which was put into effect in the academic years 1983–84 did not accomplish much because of the following factors:

(a) The short-term planning that took place on an annual basis.

(b) The limited use of mass media.
(c) Lack of legislation for compulsory education.
(d) The limited number of literacy centers opened in rural areas where illiteracy reached nearly 93.8% of the female population in some villages.[16]
(e) The limited number of qualified teachers who were trained to teach adult illiterates.

THE FIVE-YEAR PLAN FOR LITERACY CAMPAIGN (1983–89)

A 5-year-plan was designed by the Ministry of Education in 1983. The plan was then put into action during the academic year 1983/84, and it is supposed to be completed in 1988/89. The main objective of the plan is to eradicate illiteracy for the entire illiterate population of Bahrain aged 10–44 years. This population totals 26,724 persons: 20,506 females and 6,218 males.

The plan was subdivided into four phases, each of the first three phases lasting for 2 years. In the first phase, students acquire the skills of reading and writing. The second phase covers an equivalent of the elementary stage of education, whereas the third covers an equivalent of an intermediate education. The final phase starts when students can join the regular secondary schools.

The outcome of the first 2 years of the plan 1983/84–1984/85 was disappointing; it did not meet the goals that were set. Many students dropped out of the program; many others did not pass the final exams and fewer students than expected were attending classes.

In a study conducted by the Ministry of Education on the causes of the high rate of drop-outs among students, the main causes were related to the conflict between work schedules and classroom hours. Most illiterates, especially males, were not able to attend classes in the afternoons or evenings. Therefore, the 5-year-plan has been modified to include morning classes for illiterate workers in different government ministries and large companies such as the oil, gas and steel companies. The Association of the Blind also participated in the campaign by providing classes for the illiterate blind using the Braille system.

The first year of the plan (1983/84) showed an increase in the number of illiterates who joined the program. The number of students who were enrolled in the first three phases reached 8,152 persons: 4,215 in the first phase, 2,854 in the second phase and 1,083 in the third phase. By the end of the year, only 5,444 of the total (4,260 females and 1,184 males) attended the final examination whereas the remaining 33% had dropped out of the program.[17]

The plan was relatively successful in regard to morning classes, which were operated during work hours. The Ministry of Electricity and Work joined the program by opening 4 classes in which 49 illiterate employees were enrolled in classes during work hours. The Ministry of Education conducted a similar program: 42 males and 4 females were enrolled in the morning classes. The Defense and Interior Ministries are planning to undertake similar literacy programs. Unfortunately, there are not many female employees working in those ministries. So, the program cannot help much in reducing the number of illiterate females in Bahrain.

The second year of the plan, 1984/85, showed a decrease in the number of those enrolled in the program. Only 3,472 (2,611 females and 861 males) joined literacy classes. Nearly 90% of the females attended afternoon classes and 10% joined morning classes.[18] Such statistics reveal that more focus on afternoon classes for females is needed.

The second year also showed that the rate of female drop-outs was relatively high. Nearly 23% of the females who attended classes dropped out from the program; this again proves that this problem is considered one of the evidences in not achieving literacy campaign goals.

Another problem facing the program planners was the low enrollment rate. While the 5-year-plan put forth as a goal to have 2880 females in the first phase for the year 1984/85, only 2008 joined the program or 70% of the number expected.[19]

However, there are some positive outcomes that were achieved in the second year of the plan:

(a) One of the women's organizations opened day-care facilities in 4 literacy centers to take care of the participants' children. Such a positive step brought an increase in the number of women with children joining literacy classes.
(b) More morning classes were opened for men and women in 3 social centers and in such major companies as the

petro-chemical and gas companies.

(c) The second year has also witnessed an increase in the number of literacy centers. Twenty-two literacy centers were opened: 15 for females and 7 for males.

(d) Another positive step was the training of 482 teachers.

(e) More awareness has been created by the media. Television and radio networks presented a series of programs that dealt with the literacy campaign.

In sum, one can say that the 1-year-plan, which took place in 1973/74 and in the years after, and the 1983/84 5-year-plan, failed to end the illiteracy problem in Bahrain. Both plans had to deal with similar problems that were not easily resolved. The formation of a national committee for adult education in 1983 did not help much either; most of its activities were limited to a handful of television interviews and lectures and one brochure on illiteracy problems.

A survey conducted by one of the women's organizations to assess the current literacy program formulated the following suggestions to improve the literacy program:[20]

(a) Reassess the present curriculum, especially the maths, English and handicrafts.

(b) Provide transportation for students.

(c) Make extensive use of audiovisual aids.

(d) Omit some subjects so the curriculum can fit within the limited hours students can attend per week.

The survey attributed the large number of female drop-outs to such factors as the inadequacy of the curriculum, the shortage of transportation, the need to do the housework and take care of children, the demands of marriage and pregnancy and the lack of child-care facilities. A sample of 236 drop-out students were interviewed and most of them suggested the following steps to improve the program's results: training the staff better, using more modern equipment and aids in class, separating different age groups, providing adequate transportation and child-care facilities and developing an up-to-date curriculum.

Towards an Overall Effective Literacy Program

Illiteracy cannot be seen as an independent phenomenon by itself; it is linked to cultural and socio-economic factors. The 5-year-plan failed to end, or even limit, illiteracy in Bahrain. The key to realizing the success of any literacy program lies in the political will of the government. Planning a literacy program requires a unified plan for compulsory education that goes hand in hand with the 5-year-plan.

As has been indicated earlier, the voluntary nature of education may be a main factor for school age drop-outs and for a high rate of illiteracy, especially among females. Table 5.3 shows some striking figures on the number of illiterate females aged 10–19 years; this number has now reached 4,171. This is nearly four times as high as the figures for illiterate males of the same age. Such figures prove that females of school age are not attending school because of cultural barriers. The promotion of compulsory education is the most important solution to overcoming this barrier.

The important factors that keep school-age females from education are related to the following:

(a) Females tend to marry early, in some cases at 11 years of age.
(b) Married girls are restricted from enrolling in school.
(c) Females are required to do a large share of house work.
(d) Females are expected to look after siblings.
(e) Male teachers are not allowed to teach young females.
(f) Parents prefer to provide education for boys rather than for girls if they have limited financial resources.

Without the aid of laws, females in rural areas will not attend school. Iraq was one of the Arab countries that passed such legislation before starting its successful literacy campaign in 1979. The Iraqi government passed a law in 1978 making schooling compulsory for all children up to the age 15. What is needed for Bahrain is the provision for a compulsory, universal, free, primary education. The government of Bahrain should pass legislation to make primary education free and compulsory, and at a later stage, it should lengthen the period of required attendance.

Before putting compulsory education legislation into effect, a plan should be set up to estimate the material and personnel needs and the cost, and to suggest a realistic and feasible program. The plan should be two-fold: in the first phase it should deal with the short term plan and stipulate compulsory education for the primary level, and in the second phase it should deal with the long term and stipulate compulsory education for the intermediate and secondary levels for both sexes.[21]

Predicting the costs of such a plan is very difficult, but an estimate can be arrived at by consulting the statistical data provided by the 1981 census. The total population of Bahrainis (aged 5–19 years) for whom the educational facilities would be provided had reached 93,709 in 1981 (Table 5.4). They formed 39.3% or two-fifths of the total population. On the other hand, the Bahraini population of 6 years and over, enrolled in primary, intermediate and secondary schools had reached 30,961 students in 1981, nearly one-third of the school-age population. To serve such a large number of students requires massive planning and a large staff, including teachers, teacher educators and administrators.

It is a costly step, and finanical resources of this magnitude

Table 5.4 *Bahraini population by age (5–19) and sex in census years (1971–81)*

Age Groups		1971	1981
5–9	M	15,487	16,126
	F	15,514	15,920
	T	31,001	32,046
10–14	M	13,911	15,231
	F	13,679	15,095
	T	27,590	30,326
15–19	M	9,990	15,434
	F	9,849	15,903
	T	19,839	31,337
Total		78,430	93,709

Sources: Statistical Abstracts 1983, op. cit., derived from Table 7, p. 17.

would not be available at present with the decrease in oil revenues all over the Gulf region. The possibility of raising the educational budget is far from a reality under such economic circumstances. In sum, a lack of funding is the main reason for not passing compulsory education legislation.

THE FIVE-YEAR LITERACY PLAN

In assessing literacy plans prior to the 5-year-plan, it was observed that many plans did not accomplish much due to such factors as the lack of legislation for compulsory education, the limited use of the mass media and the lack of qualified personnel. The 5-year-plan, as the previous plans, failed to end the illiteracy problem in Bahrain because it viewed illiteracy as an independent phenomenon by itself, an isolated problem, not related to the overall development. Besides issuing legislation for compulsory education, the key to realizing the success of the 5-year-literacy-plan lies in implementing the following: the use of the mass media, the training of the staff for literacy programs, the full participation of women's associations, and the provision of funding for the plan. The previous issues will be discussed in the following section:

The use of the mass media

Literacy in one sense is an audiovisual process, involving the mastery of visual signs of significant sounds, and television is an audiovisual tool, which offers particular advantages in teaching an audio-visual technique.[22]

Radio is not easy to use for direct literacy instruction because of the complex skills required to coordinate locally-provided reading matter with the radio broadcast in an integrated form of radio-vision program.[23]

At present, television is more popular and most promising; it permits the use of all forms of audio-visual aids in a compact and coordinated manner. Some studies have proved that 83% is learnt through sight, as against only 11% through hearing, but 50% of what is seen and heard is retained, as against just 20% of what is heard only.[24]

Television can provide a qualified teacher for all learning groups. But the use of video-tape is the most successful and the efficient method in television use. A qualified teacher can record his best and most polished performance on vido-tape through the extensive preparation and revision of each lesson with the help of micro-testing and feedback.

Using television for literacy programs in Bahrain

Many countries started using television for literacy purposes in the early 1960s. Such use was restricted to small, rather than massive operations.

Italy was among the countries that utilized television in literacy programs from 1960 to 1968 with its program 'It's Never Too Late'. The drop in the number of illiterates was great. As many as 1.5 million viewed the program. Mexico also started using television in 1965 in its literacy campaign under the heading of 'I Can Do it'. From 1966–68, radio and television helped 2 million people. Such Arab countries as Egypt and Tunisia utilized television in literacy campaigns in the 1960s, and the programs were reported to have been successful.[25]

Bahrain and the other Gulf states will be utilizing television and radio in literacy programs in the near future. A literacy program called 'An-Al-Awan', which means 'On The Move', is under completion in Kuwait. The series will consist of 56 lessons. Each lesson will last for 30 minutes. The program will be broadcast four times a week for 6 months and will cover the first phase of the literacy campaign, which consists of learning the basic skills of reading, writing and maths. The contents of the program will be related to various aspects of the daily life of the learners. Such different forms of learning will be used as skits, documentary films, songs, music and cartoons presented with the help of audio-visual aids. The language that will be used is Arabic.

The program is funded by the Arabic Fund for Social and Economic Development and the Arab Fund for Literacy and Adult Education. The program is produced by the Arab Gulf Joint Production Institute, based in Kuwait. It will be telecast in early 1988; and it will also be on video-cassettes.

The women who would benefit most from the television and video literacy programs are those who could not otherwise be reached outside their homes.

In order to assure more success for the program, the following recommendations should be put into consideration:

1. Besides using video-cassettes at home, learners should watch a well-run daily half-hour literacy program on television.
2. Televisions and video sets should be provided for those who still don't own one. The TV set is essential to the project. Through the Ministry of Education, television and video sets should be provided for students, especially for female students. An amount of money could be contributed by the authorities toward the purchase of televisions and videos.
3. Female students should not have to leave home every day. They could study their lessons on the video-cassette and go to the literacy center once or twice a week to consult the supervisor.
4. A joint team from the Ministry of Education and the television network should share the responsibility of telecasting the program in ordr to avoid pitfalls and assure success of the program.

The feasibility of going beyond the pilot stage to an extensive application will be decided after the completion of the first 6 months.

Training of literacy staff

The training of personnel to work with illiterates plays a major role in the success of any literacy program. Developing an appropriate training system requires a great effort because the training of personnel to eradicate illiteracy is quite different from the training of school teachers. People who work with illiterates have to mobilize the learners and the community and to organize community resources for the program. Motivation, participation and coordination are very important in literacy programs and in adult education.[26]

Training personnel to work with illiterates requires a knowledge of adult psychology and adult learning behaviour. The curriculum for primary education differs a great deal from the curriculum for adult literacy programs. The first is subject-oriented, whereas the second is more flexible to meet the needs of learners. It also has to start from the experiences of the learners.[27]

Television and video-cassettes could be used more effectively to train teachers in a training program. Teachers could be guided and become well informed about new methods, especially audio-visual techniques, which are effectively demonstrated by television and video-cassettes.

People who are involved in the literacy campaign in Bahrain have realized that the training of staff, including field workers, instructors, supervisors and administrators has become of vital importance for the success of the program. The Director of Adult Education in Bahrain has proposed a plan to train people working with illiterates.[28] The plan calls for classifying the staff into two groups: teachers and administrators, and it suggests different kinds of training programs, varying from long-term to short-term training sessions, seminars and workshops. He also suggests that priorities in training should be given to the supervisors of literacy centers because of their direct responsibility to register students and to provide all kinds of equipment and books for the staff in different literacy centers.[29]

The Regional Literacy Training Center in Bahrain

A center for training staff for adult education was established in 1977 in Bahrain. This regional center is part of the main literacy center based in Iraq and is a part of the Arab League Organization. The center has already organized and conducted 24 seminars and training sessions all over the Gulf states in the last 8 years. The duration of each session varies in length from 4 days to 5 months; the average is 3 weeks for each session.

Since the center's establishment in 1977 until the present, Bahrain seems to be among the Gulf states that has benefited most from the center's activities. Table 5.5 shows that the number of Bahrainis who have participated in the training sessions has reached 229 (out of a total of 444 persons from all over the Gulf region).

An interesting fact is shown in Table 5.5 the number of Bahraini females who participated in the training sessions has reached 170 or 38.4% of the total. Thus, having the Regional Center in Bahrain has helped, to a great extent, in the training of those working with illiterates. More important, its location has reduced the cost of the training plan.

The center is located in an old compound that lacks many facilities. These deficiencies vary from poor ventilation, insuffi-

Table 5.5 *Percentage of participants in the training sessions by sex and nationality (1977–84)*

	Sex		
Nationality	male (%)	female (%)	total (%)
UAE	3.8	0.7	4.5
Bahrain	13.2	38.4	51.6
Saudi Arabia	12.6	—	12.6
Oman	5.2	0.4	5.6
Iraq	4.5	—	4.5
Qatar	9.0	—	9.0
Kuwait	7.9	2.3	10.2
Jordan	1.8	0.2	2.0
Total	58	42	100

Source: Al-Alawi, Hashim, op. cit., derived from Table 5, p. 11.

cient audio-visual aids and equipment, to unqualified personnel and a poor library. Nevertheless, the Center has proved to serve the interests of Bahrain in the training of personnel working with illiterates more than any other Gulf state. Thus, the government of Bahrain is more likely to provide the Center with better services by: offering a new modern facility, purchasing adequate equipment and audio-visual aids and improving the quality of personnel who work at the Center.

Full Participation of Women's Associations

Eradicating illiteracy cannot be accomplished by government efforts alone. The participation and coordination of different social groups and women's associations is required to make the literacy campaign more successful.

Women's associations play an important role in the literacy campaign, especially among illiterate females who are at the core of the illiteracy problem. They can help in creating more awareness among illiterate females in villages, in planning literacy programs, in coordinating efforts between students and staff members, and in providing facilities for classes in different locations. Also, volunteers from women's associations could be trained as teachers, and could help reduce the teacher shortage.

They can bring the illiteracy problem to public awareness by organizing seminars and lectures.

In Bahrain, teaching illiterate females is a major objective for many women's associations. Many have participated in literacy programs since the 1960s when the An-Nahdhah Women's Association opened literacy classes and many members of the society participated in the teaching. In 1970, the number of females who joined classes reached 87. The Child & Mother Welfare Association followed in 1963. Ten years later, the number of women who had joined classes reached 80. The Awal Women's Association also joined in teaching illiterate females in 1970. At present, members of the association are recruiting teachers and paying their salaries in one literacy center. Furthermore, they are organizing lectures and other educational programs for female students in various literacy centers. In four literacy centers, they also helped illiterate mothers with children by providing day-care centers to take care of their children during classtime.[30]

In general, the women's associations in Bahrain could be classified as voluntary associations working for the women's cause. However, the main role for women's associations in Bahrain is creating more awareness within the local communities and, thus, encouraging more illiterate females to join literacy classes.

Funding

The 5-year-plan was estimated to cost nearly 20 m Bahraini Dinars, an amount equivalent to $50 m. The Ministry of Education is not able to cover the cost because of limited resources. Therefore, the cost of the literacy campaign together with the cost of compulsory education could be funded by three main sources:

1. The Arab Gulf Program for UN Development Organizations.
2. The Islamic Charity Funds (Waqf).
3. The Arab Fund for Literacy and Adult Education.

Those three funding sources will be discussed in detail to assess their feasibility.

Arab Gulf Program for UN Development Organizations (AGFUND)

AGFUND was established in 1981 by the Arab gulf states and is headed by Prince Talal Bin Abdul-Aziz Al-Saud of Saudi Arabia. In its first year of operating, AGFUND participated in financing 38 programs in 31 countries all over Africa, Asia and Latin America. The cost of these programs reached $34,799,000. Furthermore, AGFUND financed many projects of the UN Organizations: $2,520,000 for FAO; $4,950,000 for UNDP; $2,320,000 for UNEP; $4,000,000 for UNESCO; $25,000,000 for UNESIF and $5,500,000 for WHO.

As for Bahrain in 1982, AGFUND financed some of its educational and health projects to the amount of $1,500,000. AGFUND is already involved in financing literacy programs in the Arab world. (It financed the literacy program in North Yemen in 1982 to the amount of $2,000,000.) In 1985, AGFUND financed the Arab Adult Literacy Organization based in Baghdad. The head of AGFUND is a strong advocate of the financing of literacy programs and child-care services. There is a good chance of funding the literacy campaign in Bahrain through AGFUND.

The Islamic Charity Fund (Waqf)

Waqf controls a great deal of wealth. Property belonging to Waqf ranges from fish traps to palm gardens and arid lands: 16.5% of the 159 fish traps in Bahrain are owned by Waqf,[31] and nearly 13% of all land plots are owned by the Waqf.[32]

This vast wealth is misused; land is distributed illegally to influential people who lease it for a period of 20–50 years with only a token amount of money that represents only 1% of its real value. There are not enough data or documents on this issue, but it is well known to the public that Waqf wealth has been exploited.

At present, part of the Waqf money is distributed to different mosques. It would be more appropriate for the government of Bahrain, through the Ministry of Justice, to modernize the Waqf laws and issue a decree in order to legalize the use of Waqf property to finance literacy programs.

The Arab Fund for Literacy and Adult Education

The fund was established in 1980 by the Arab League

Educational, Cultural and Scientific Organisation (ALESCO) to participate in financing the plans of generalizing compulsory primary education as well as literacy and adult education projects, in the Arab countries. The fund aims at contributing to the building up of the necessary infrastructure that would help the Arab states launch a comprehensive effort to achieve full literacy. The fund has already contributed to 11 programs on literacy in different Arab countries with an estimated cost of between $90,000 to more than $10,000,000 for each project. The fund would most likely approve of funding the literacy program in Bahrain.

Conclusion

Education has a great influence on changing the situation of women. As mentioned earlier, census data, as well as studies conducted in many countries, including Bahrain, indicate a strong correlation between the level of female literacy and the access of women to the labor market: the higher the female illiteracy rates, the lower the women's participation in the labor force.

The programs initiated in Bahrain to eradicate illiteracy failed to achieve this because they viewed illiteracy as an independent phenomenon, one on its own and not related to the overall development. We have suggested that legislation for compulsory education should be passed before initiating the literacy program. The program will also include instruction in the best use of mass media, training personnel for literacy programs, full participation of women's association and provisions for the funding of both the literacy program and compulsory education. Such procedures would make literacy programs more successful. Furthermore, the present educational system would be more capable of producing the future labor force of the economy. For such an objective, there should be more coordination between education and literacy programs. Many positive results are achieved from such coordination. The first joint effort is of a financial nature. The functioning on a parallel basis of different programs, which have similar objectives, can be very costly. The second effort is to ensure that literacy be considered as an initial stage in a wider educational process. Therefore students who are joining literacy programs have the possibility of continuing from one form of education to another.

Notes

1. The UNESCO *Courier Magazine*, Feb. 1984, p. 3.
2. *Statistical Abstracts/1984*, State of Bahrain, Council of Ministers, Central Statistics Organization (Dec. 1985) p. 134.
3. Emile A. Nakhleh, *Bahrain* (Mass.: Lexington Books, 1976) p. 21.
4. Ismael Sergeldin, James A. Socnat, Stace Birks, Bob Li and Clive A. Sinclair, *Manpower and International Labor Migration in the Middle East and North Africa* (World Bank publication), Oxford University Press, 1983, p. 41.
5. J. S. Birks and J. A. Rimmer, *Developing Education Systems in The Oil States of Arabia: Conflicts of Purposes and Focus*, Occasional papers series No. 21, manpower and migration series No. 3, Centre for Middle Eastern and Islamic Studies, University of Durham, England, 1984, p. 5.
6. Ibid., p. 6.
7. Ibid., p. 13.
8. Nadia Youssef, 'Education and Female Modernism in the Muslim World', *Journal of International Affairs*, vol. 30, no. 2, 1977, p. 206.
9. Lubna A. Al-Kazi, *The Impact of Education on Women's Economic Participation: A Case Study of Kuwaiti Women*, paper presented to The Regional Planning Conference for Arab Women, Nicosia, Cyprus (24–29 June 1985). Organized by the Institute of Women's studies in the Arab World, Beirut, Lebanon, 1985, p. 12.
10. Byron Masialas and Jamila Mikati, *Strategies for Educating Arab Women to Participate in National Development*, paper presented to the Regional Planning Conference for Arab Women, Nicosia, Cyprus, (24–29 June 1985). Organized by the Institute of Women's Studies in the Arab World, Beirut, Lebanon, 1985, p. 18.
11. *Backgrounder: Literacy Education*, UNESCO, Paris, June 1983, p. 3.
12. Marcel de Clerck, 'Where There's a Will. . .', The UNESCO *Courier Magazine* (Feb. 1984), p. 9.
13. Anita Dighe, 'Programs with Focus on Women's involvement: the Case of India', in Bordia, A. and Carron, G. (Eds), *Issues in Planning and Implementing National Literacy Programs*, UNESCO, Paris, 1985, p. 150.
14. G. Carron and A. Bordia, 'Introduction', in Bordia, A. and Carron, G. (Eds), op. cit., p. 19.

15. M. Ahmed, M. Fares Alkhalifa, A. Darrah, *Waqi' Albaramej almutatawerah lemahwel-ummeyah wata-aleem alkibar bel-Bahrain* (programs for adult education in Bahrain), Bahrain, 1983 (Arabic), pp. 11–12.
16. *A Field Study on Women's Illiteracy in Bahrain*, An-Nahdha Women's Society, 1983 (Arabic), p. 176.
17. M. Abbas Ahmed, M. F. Alkhalifa, a. Darrah, *Waqi' albaramej almutatawerah lemahwel-ummeyah wata-aleem alkibar bel-Bahrain* (programs for adult education in Bahrain), Bahrain, 1983 (Arabic), pp. 11–12.
18. Ministry of Education, Department of Adult Education, *Ass-sana athaniya min al-khutta alkhamsiya limahewl ummiyah: ardh wa tahleel* (The second year of the five-year plan: an assessment), Bahrain, June 1985 (Arabic), p. 2.
19. Ibid., p. 16.
20. *Dirasah mydaniya howla waqi' al-ummiya bidoulatel-Bahrain* (a field study on women's illiteracy in Bahrain). An-Nahdha women's society (Arabic), 1983, p. 141.
21. UNESCO, *The Needs of Asia in Primary Education*, educational studies and documents, no. 41, Paris, 1961, p. 9.
22. John Maddison, *Radio and Television in Literacy*, a survey of the use of the broadcasting media in combatting illiteracy among adults, UNESCO, Paris, 1971, p. 33.
23. Rafi-uz-zaman, 'Innovative Methods in the Use of Mass Media: Utilizing Television for Functional Literacy', in Carron, G., and Bordia, A. (Eds), op. cit., p. 225.
24. Ibid., p. 225.
25. Rafi-uz-Zaman, op. cit., p. 229.
26. A. Chiba, 'Training of Illiteracy Personnel: Experience of the UNESCO Regional Office for Education in Asia and the Pacific', in Carron, G., and Bordia, A. (Eds), op. cit., p. 274.
27. Ibid., p. 275.
28. M. Abbas Ahmed, *Report No. 4 regarding a plan to train literacy workers*, Ministry of Education, Bahrain (Feb. 1983).
29. Ibid., p. 11.
30. Aisha Matar, *Dourel-jam'iyat At-tatow-o'iyah fi harakat mahwel-Ummya bedowal alkhalij* (The role of voluntary associations in eradicating illiteracy in the Gulf states), Paper presented to the training session for women's associations leaders, Bahrain, (27 October–1 November 1984). Organized by Adult Education Training Center for the Gulf States, Bahrain.
31. Foud Khuri, *Tribe and State in Bahrain: The Transformation of Social and Political Authority in an Arab State*, op. cit., p. 55.
32. Ibid., Table 2, p. 42.

Chapter Six

Vocational Training for Females

> Perhaps the greatest constraint on improving women's access to training leading to marketable skills for employment (or training which can be used to good effect in self-employment) is the difficulty of knowing how to break into a vicious circle. Perceived social roles for women influence the type and nature of education they receive, which in turn affect their view of themselves and the jobs to which they might aspire.[1]

Interest in vocational training and non-formal education in general has increased tremendously in recent years in Bahrain, because the inherent limitations of formal education have become evident. Non-formal education programs, which range from individualized apprenticeships to nationwide literacy programs, are supported to serve several needs: as an alternative for those who lack the opportunity to acquire formal education; as an extension of formal schooling for those who need additional training to get better employment; and as a means of upgrading the skills of those already employed.

It would be unrealistic to rely on formal education as a major contribution for changing the situation of women in Bahrain. What is needed is more emphasis on education and training outside the formal educational structure in order to reach the majority of women. Thus, vocational training is considered an important aspect of the non-formal education system that would help more females to join the labor market. Such training could be offered on two levels: the first level is usually associated with non-academic intermediate or secondary-school levels, which would require previous education; the second level is directed more at the non-elite female population with minimum education.[2]

However, education and training continue to operate in a

traditional way regardless of changing needs, a situation of which policy makers are aware, but they are too slow to respond to changes and new challenges.

In order to strengthen female vocational training, three points should be taken into consideration:[3]

1. The first point is that the effectiveness of the training system and the use of resources for training could be seriously damaged by a lack of coordination. This lack exists between the training systems, the formal education system and the market for skills produced through training. This problem affects all training systems for both sexes.
2. The second point is the importance of vocational guidance and counselling during and after formal education. Such guidance is very crucial in helping to shape the future role of females in society, in educating the community on the need to encourage women and men to play an equal role in society and the economy, and in changing traditional attitudes regarding the role of both sexes inside the home and in working life.

   Vocational guidance is also required for women who face dificulty when returning to work after having a family. The absence of vocational guidance linked to training and retraining will act as a major constraint on their access to more highly skilled jobs and may deprive them of any opportunity for career development.
3. The third point deals with the nature and content of training. Women's participation rate in technical and vocational training for employable skills is very low in areas of priority for development programs. The type of training offered to women often has no relevance to the manpower requirement of the labor market, yet it is the type of training that influences employability, quality of employment and earning capacity.

THE GROWING NEED FOR VOCATIONAL TRAINING FOR WOMEN IN BAHRAIN

Technical manpower in Bahrain could be grouped into the following categories:

(a) High level professional: engineers, accountants, supervisors, etc. who are trained in universities.
(b) Technicians: an intermediate grade of workers normally trained in polytechnics and colleges of technology.
(c) Skilled workers: workers who are trained through apprentices, or by a combination of formal vocational education and apprenticeship. Such training is conducted at technical training colleges or industrial vocational institutes.
(d) Semi-skilled workers: workers who may receive short vocational training or who may learn on the job without any formal training.
(e) Unskilled labor: workers who are used for positions requiring no formal training.

Prior to 1975, few nationals occupied the first category (high level professional), whereas more filled the fourth and fifth categories (semi-skilled and unskilled workers). However, with the expansion of the economy in 1975, following the sharp increase in oil revenues, shortages of trained manpower were identified as a major obstacle to the Bahrain economic development. This skill scarcity has arisen from two interrelated factors: the orientation of Bahrain's education system towards the arts and literature; and the limited opportunities for vocational and technical training, especially for females.

Although considerable improvement has been made in the educational system, a large proportion of labor force entrants continues to fall short of meeting the higher occupational requirements of the economy. At the beginning of 1975, with the expansion of the economy. manpower planners recognized that there was a severe shortage of technical and skilled manual workers. Table 6.1 shows the magnitude of dependency on foreign workers by economic sector. In 1975 non-nationals were more present in three sectors particularly: the manufacturing, service and construction sectors. These exhibited a high level of dependency on foreign workers. In the same year, their employment accounted for 44% in construction, 42% in services and 41% in manufacturing. This percentage was projected by World Bank experts to increase in 1985 to reach 63.3% in construction, 53.7% in services and 50.4% in manufacturing. Furthermore, in the agricultural sector, which is considered the

Table 6.1 *Non-nationals' share of employment by economic sector, 1975 and 1985 (%)*

Economic Sector	Employment 1975 (%)	Employment 1985 (%)
1. Agriculture	27.0	30.9
2. Mining and Quarrying	35.1	49.7
3. Manufacturing	41.0	50.0
4. Utilities	8.6	26.7
5. Construction	44.0	63.3
6. Trade and Finance	32.5	56.5
7. Transport and Communications	32.9	48.7
8. Services	42.0	53.7
Total	37	53.9

Sources: Serageldin, I. et al., *Manpower and International Labor Migration in the Middle East and North Africa*, op. cit., derived from Table 4-6, p. 33.

traditional sector, foreign worker participation was 27% in 1975 and projected to increase to 30.9% in 1985. The trade and finance sector showed greater increases in foreign workers from 32.5% in 1975 to 56.5% in 1985.[4]

No statistics are available for the year 1985 to prove the accuracy of the previous projections; however, statistics derived from the 1981 census indicated that the proportion of foreign workers in the previously mentioned sectors reached even higher levels than the projected numbers for the year 1985. The proportion of foreign workers increased in the construction sector to 86.8%, in the service sector to 52.9% and in the manufacturing sector to 66.3%.[5] With the recent recession in the economy caused by the oil glut and the decrease in oil revenues, the proportion of foreign workers is more likely to decrease. But no one expects a sharp decrease in the near future. On the contrary, it would be more likely that unemployment among nationals might increase because of their lack of skills needed in the modern sectors of the economy.

The needs will rise substantially for higher levels of skill among foreign workers. The overall pattern of rising requirements for more highly trained workers is shown in Table 6.2. Professional

Table 6.2 *Non-nationals' employment by occupational level, 1975 and 1985 (number in thousands)*

Occupational Level	Employment 1975		Employment 1985	
	No.	%	No.	%
1) Professional and Technical (9A–1)	0.5	1.7%	2.3	2.8%
2) Other Professional (A–2)	1.9	6.5%	6.2	7.7%
3) Sub-professional and Technical (B–1)	0.9	3.1%	2.7	3.3%
4) Other Sub-professional (B–2)	0.0	0.0	6.6	8.1%
5) Skilled Office and Manual (C–1)	12.7	43.7%	37.3	45.9%
6) Semi-skilled Office and Manual (C–2)	7.6	26.1%	12.7	15.6%
7) Unskilled	5.5	18.9%	13.5	16.6%
Total	29.1	100.0	81.3	100.0

Sources: Serageldin, I., et al., *Manpower and International Labor Migration in the Middle East and North Africa*, op. cit., derived from Table 4-8, p. 34.

occupations (A–1, A–2) accounted for 8.2% (2,400) of all employment in 1975, and by 1985 this proportion is projected to rise to 10.5% (5,500). In contrast, the proportion of unskilled foreign workers will decrease from 18.9% in 1975 to 16.6% in 1985, although their number will increase from 5,500 to 13,500 for the same period. In other sub-professional and technical areas (B–1, B–2) the proportion of foreign workers accounted for only 3.1% (900) in 1975 and was projected to rise to 11.4% (9,300) in 1985. Yet, the large increase in non-nationals will occur mainly in skilled and semi-skilled office and manual jobs (C–1, C–2) where the proportion reached 69.8% (19,300) in 1975 and was projected to reach 61.5% (50,000) in 1985. Table 6.2 reflects the areas in which foreign workers are mostly concentrated. It also indicates that the need for vocational training for nationals is mostly needed in the sub-professional, skilled, semi-skilled and manual jobs.

Although educational attainment and economic necessity have encouraged a larger number of females to seek employment,

Table 6.3 *Economically active population, 15 years and over, by occupation, nationality and sex, 1981*

Occupation	Nationality/Sex Bahraini M	F	T	Non-Bahraini M	F	T	Nationality/Sex Total M	F	T
1. Profession, Technical and Related Workers	4,827	3,396	8,396	6,441	1,628	8,069	11,268	5,024	16,292
2. Administrative and Managerial Workers	798	40	838	1,260	42	1,302	2,058	82	2,140
3. Clerical and Related Workers	9,118	3,255	12,373	4,229	1,168	5,397	13,347	4,423	17,770
4. Sales Workers	4,865	105	4,970	4,629	85	4,714	9,494	190	9,684
5. Service Workers	7,381	851	8,232	14,717	3,737	18,454	22,089	4,588	26,686
6. Agricultural, Animal Husbandry and Forestry Workers, Fishermen and Hunters	2,799	6	2,805	2,228	3	2,231	5,027	9	5,036
7. Production and Related Workers, Transport Equipment Operators and Laborers	19,266	198	19,464	40,389	130	40,519	59,655	328	59,983
8. Laborers not Elsewhere Classified	1,612	20	1,632	3,306	21	3,327	4,918	41	4,959
9. Not Stated	479	41	520	36	6	42	515	47	562
10. Not Applicable	2,927	4,284	7,211	419	350	769	3,346	4,634	7,980
Grand Total	52,460	12,176	64,636	74,348	7,149	81,497	126,808	19,325	146,133

Sources: Bahrain census of population & housing 1981, op. cit., derived from Table 33, pp. 71–86.

there has not been a comprehensive attempt to direct women's employment in sectors experiencing labor shortages. Table 6.3 illustrates the economically active population classified by occupation, nationality and sex in 1981:

1. Clerical workers and workers in related occupations account for a total of 17,700; Bahraini female workers account for only 18.4% of the total, whereas foreign workers account for 30.4% of the total.
2. Sales workers total 9,684; Bahraini female workers constitute 1% only, whereas foreign workers account for nearly 49% of the total.
3. Service workers account for a total of 26,686, Bahraini female workers constitute 3% and foreign workers 70%.

Such statistics reflect the great demand for more vocational training. They also indicate that vocational secondary schools cannot respond effectively to the short term labor market demand, for example, only 407 males graduated from such schools in 1983/84. Females are excluded from attending industrial schools altogether. Their enrollment in this field is limited to the commercial secondary schools, which they started to join in 1970/71. By 1980, their number had increase to reach 600 females, equal to that of their male counterpart.

Therefore, secondary schools for vocational training and other existing programs are unlikely to meet labor shortages. In addition, the growing number of the unemployed among the unskilled points to the need for an expansion of the existing vocational training programs. The encouragement of females to join vocational training programs will not only increase the number of technically and professionally qualified females, but it will also reduce the dependence on foreign labor as well.

BARRIERS AFFECTING WOMEN'S PARTICIPATION IN VOCATIONAL TRAINING PROGRAMS

No major legal barriers to women's vocational training exist in Bahrain. But women's participation and options are still severely limited. Large numbers of females remain completely out of training systems, whereas funds are invested in training women in jobs for which there is no demand. Most of the programs that exist are limited to certain traditional skills related to women's role as housewives. Such skills include training for sewing and handicrafts. The Ministry of Labor and Social Affairs, for instance, is sponsoring a program to teach female participants sewing and handicrafts. This program has not been very successful because the majority of the participants have failed to find work after completing the program. This suggests that education and training continue to operate in a mechanical way and that training should be linked to the skills needed in the labor market.

Because of social norms, vocational training opportunities for females are limited in scope and do not allow for entry into diverse activities. In addition, the attitude of society as a whole regarding education and training play an important role in influencing the education and occupational choice of young females. Even if females are free to undergo education and training, they may not be able to do so for various reasons. There may be a lack of the proper vocational training institutions. Women may not take advantage of training opportunities because traditional attitudes prevent them from acquiring skills necessary for modern jobs. Furthermore, females sometimes acquire certain skills that are not in demand in the labor market. Their training is oriented towards only a few occupations, away from those in the industrial fields and towards those in the social sector including teaching, nursing and social welfare.

The low level of literacy among females (discussed in the previous chapter) is a major barrier that keeps many away from the labor market. Illiterate females constitute 80% of the overall illiterates aged 10–44 years in Bahrain.

Another important barrier that prevents women from improving their access to training is that the perceived social roles for women influence the type and nature of education they receive, which in turn affects their view of themselves and of the jobs to which they might aspire. The choice of vocational options at the secondary school level for girls remains very limited to such traditionally oriented courses as nursing, home economics and secretarial skills. This makes it more clear that female nationals are unlikely to fill the labor shortages, and the increase of foreign labor may limit further increases in females labor force participation.

RELATED EXISTING PROGRAMS IN BAHRAIN

Vocational training started in Bahrain in 1975 as a result of the acute manpower shortages following the expansion of the economy in the 1970s. Some large private and semi-public companies such as Bahrain Petroleum, Bahrain Telecommunication and Aluminium Bahrain were exempted from levy and established their own training centers to train their employees according to the companies' needs.

However, smaller private companies were not able to follow suit and train their employees. The government started to take a leading role in vocational training and formed the High Council for Vocational Training in 1975. This council consists of three divisions representing the government, employers and employees. It provides plans and design policies for training and coordinating. Then the Manpower Development Directorate was established in 1976. Training was carried out for such vocational trades as welding, carpentry, auto mechanics, masonry and concrete work, air conditioning and refrigeration and fabrication. The duration of each training session was between 4 and 6 months. In 1980, a training center was established, providing training in the banking field.

By the end of 1980, the Directorate of Manpower Development formed a unit called '10,000 training plan unit'. This unit conducted courses in the areas of administration, accounting, computer, clerical and secretarial work and engineering. The courses were held at the Gulf College for Technology and at other training institutes. In 1981, a three-year Apprenticeship Training Program was established. Another expansion followed in 1982 when the evening classes for the Vocational Training Program were held at Isa Town Training Center for a duration of two years. In addition to those programs, other programs limited to females were established in the last decade to develop the skills and abilities of women as a way of improving their educational and economic standards. Such projects include sewing, hair styling and a productive family program that aims to maintain such local industries as palm leaf products and pottery. These programs will be discussed and assessed in detail below.

Training for 10,000 Bahrainis

A study was conducted by the Ministry of Labor and Social Affairs in 1979 to assess the needs for manpower. The study indicated that there were 11,000 jobs filled by non-nationals in the middle and high occupational levels and suggested that the reason Bahrainis were not holding such jobs was their lack of skills. Such occupations were classified into four categories.[6]

1. Management, supervision, accounting and professions including medicine and engineering.
2. Middle level occupations.
3. Clerical middle level and related occupations.
4. Handicraft skills.

As a result of that study, a plan was made to train Bahrainis to replace foreign labor filling such jobs. The plan was called 'training plan for 10,000 Bahrainis', and set a goal to provide vocational training and educational sessions for approximately 10,000 Bahraini employees working in the private sector within a period of 10 years. The program would start in 1981 with the objective of training 1,000 to 1,250 each year.

The primary goal of the plan was to assist employers in developing the skills of Bahraini employees to their full potential. The training was also available to unemployed persons to develop and improve their skills. The plan also sponsored students in a variety of training courses at several schools including the Gulf College for Technology, Polyglot School and Bahrain Management Institute. The courses covered the following: management studies, clerical supervision, accounting, electrical, mechanical and engineering technicians, travel, insurance, computer programming, data processing and secretarial studies.

Evaluation of the First 5 Years of the Plan (1981–86):

At the beginning, the program was funded by the government, this lasted until the end of 1983. Then 50% of the funding came from the High Council for Training, whereas the government covered the other half of the budget. By 1985, the entire program was funded through the private sector represented by the High Council for Training. In 1981 the budget was nearly $700,000 and continued increasing until it reached $1,300,000 in 1986.

Employers were supposed to release students one day per week to attend classes. Other class sessions were held in the evening. The duration of the courses ranged from a year for clerical supervision courses to 3 years for engineering technician courses. All courses require the participants to have a high school diploma and to be able to read and write English.

More than 5 years after it was implemented, the plan failed to reach its goals. Statistics indicate that the number of graduates lag far behind the goals that were set to train 1,000 to 1,250 each year. Those who joined the program in the first year (1981) numbered 688 out of 1589 applicants: 43.3% of the trainees passed their exam. Most of those trained in management, accounting and computer programming. As for clerical and secretrial training participants, 71.3% were females and 95% of them were unemployed.

The number of those accepted in the program started to decrease over time, and many did not pass or dropped out. Table 6.4 indicates that the proportion of females in the program reached 37.4% (315) in 1982. However, in 1983/84 the proportion of females increased to 46.4% (312) of the total. A year later, females formed 50% (297) of the total. By 1985/86 the female enrollment decreaseed to 47% of the total (408).

Yet, despite its increase in the clerical and secretarial sector, female participation was very small in the supervisory and management sector (Table 6.5). In the first year of the program, females constituted less than 1.5% of the total. However, the grand total of females in the last 5 years in this sector was 302 or only 13% of the total.

Table 6.6 indicates that the overall enrollment of females increased substantially in 1985/86. Females formed 40.5% (234) of the total. Their numbers were concentrated in bookkeeping, secretarial work, office practice and data processing, whereas their proportion in management and supervision decreased dramatically, and it disappeared in engineering: mechanical, electrical and instrumentation.

Many factors contributed to the program's failure to achieve its goals. One factor was the relatively high drop-out rate of the trainees: 37% (482) dropped-out in 1981, and 20% in 1982. The drop-out rate could be related to the trainees, employers and the curriculum:[7]

Table 6.4 *Enrollment in the training plan for 10,000 Bahraini by occupational status, specialization and sex*

Specialization/ Type of Course	Occupational Status						Total
	Employed			Unemployed			
	M	F	T	M	F	T	
1. Clerical work	21	15	36	18	66	84	120
2. Insurance	7	—	7	8	2	10	17
3. Travel	7	6	13	12	8	20	33
4. Bookkeeping	50	28	78	29	23	52	130
5. Accounting	31	12	43	2	—	2	45
6. Management	62	4	66	1	—	1	67
7. Office supervision	43	24	67	5	1	6	73
8. Data processing	55	35	90	32	35	67	157
9. Mechanical engineering	47	—	47	5	—	5	52
10. Electrical Engineering	32	—	32	13	—	13	45
11. Construction technicians	5	4	9	10	10	4	23
12. Instrumentation	31	—	31	—	—	—	31
13. Power plant operator	1	—	1	—	—	—	1
14. Secretarial	—	—	—	—	48	48	48
Total	392	128	520	135	187	322	842

Sources: Zuraiqat, Sami *Training Plan for 10,000 Bahrainis: in Its 3rd Year: an assessment*, op. cit., derived from Table 12, p. 20.

Table 6.5 *Total number of enrollments, drop-outs and passing in the supervisory and management training program during the period 1980–85*

Years	Passing	Drop-outs	Enrollments	Male	Female
1980	301	37	338	333	5
1981	330	79	409	311	98
1982	382	31	413	343	70
1983	458	32	490	443	47
1984	283	30	313	274	39
1985	330	18	348	305	43
Grand total	2084	227	2311	2009	302

Sources: Directorate of Manpower Development, Planning and Evaluation section, 1986

Table 6.6 *10,000 plan students attendance Oct. 1985–Feb. 1986*

Course	Enrolled				Withdrew			
	M	F	T	%	M	F	T	%
Adv. management 1	24	2	26	—	—	—		
Mid. management	24	2	26	8	2	—	2	
Basic super.	23	2	25	8	2	—	2	
Clerical level	11	8	19	42	1	2	3	
Bookkeeping 1	70	25	95	26	13	8	21	
Accounting	16	7	23	30	1	—	1	
Secretarial	—	33	33	100	—	—	—	
Engineering Tech	58	—	58	0	2	—	2	
Mechanical	20	—	20	0	—	—	—	
Electrical	17	—	17	0	1	—	1	
Instrumentation	9	—	9	0		—	—	
Data Processing	25	20	45	44	7	5	12	
Data Processing computer	15	15	30	50	1	—	1	
Programming	17	3	20	15	—	—	—	
Office Practice	—	65	56	100	—	2	2	
Secretarial studies	—	26	26	100	—	—	—	
Insurance	9	9	18	50	—	—	—	
Travel	6	17	23	30	—	—	—	
Total	344	234	578		29	18	47	

Sources: Directorate of Manpower Development, Planning and Evaluation Section, Ministry of Labor and Social Affairs, 1986

1. Trainees joined the program in order to improve their skills and their job positions. After joining the program, they realized that they did not have enough time to accomplish both their work and training at the same time. As a result, they chose to drop-out and keep their jobs.
2. Employers created many obstacles for the trainees to make them stop training during work time. Employers did not provide transportation for the trainees to go to training centers. In addition, trainees were asked to work extra hours to make up for the time spent in training. In addition to this, some large companies had their own training programs. This made them stop sending trainees to join the program.
3. As for the curriculum, most courses were taught in English, which most of the trainees did not speak well. This made the program unappealing to them. The

curriculum in general had been borrowed from foreign academic institutions without any modification to fit the local market needs.

Apprenticeship Training Program

Traditionally, an apprenticeship meant training in a manual craft. Today, the word is still used in the same sense, although the concept has been broadened to include similar activities in technical and commerical occupations. It is a form of training that combines practical experience on the shop floor with theoretical learning at schools or in other institutions, and full-time academic vocational training by attending courses in special centers within the general system of education.

In 1981, a 3-year Apprenticeship Training Program was established at Isa Town Training Center. The program consists of a year of training at the Training Center, followed by 2 years of 'on-the-job' training within the company and 'off-the-job' training within the Vocational Training Center at Isa Town. The first year of training is divided into three periods and is based on 50% workshop practice, 20% related theory and 30% academic subjects, which include mathematics, science and communication skills. The purpose of 'on-the-job' training is to provide an opportunity for apprentices who have satisfactorily completed basic training to gain relevant work experience within production units. Apprentices must be released 2 days a week in order to attend classes in academic subjects at the training center.

The program recruits apprentices not older than 18 years of age who have completed the 9th grade of schooling. The program coordinates theoretical and practical training, monitors progress, reports about training and supervises testing. Furthermore, the program covers nine specializations.

The program is financed by the High Council for Vocational Training, which was originally funded by the private sector. The program's budget increased from nearly $1 m in 1983 to $2 m in 1984. The average cost per trainee ranges from $6,000 in the first year, $2,600 in the second year and $3,600 in the third year. However, regardless of the high cost of training, the program seems successful and is expanding each year. Table 6.7 illustrates the number of apprentices enrolled in the 3-year apprenticeship program of the year 1983/84. It shows that the number of

Table 6.7 *Apprentices enrolled in 3 years of apprenticeship program by specialization, 1983–1984*

Specialization	First year	Second year	Third year
1. Building Electricians	26	25	14
2. Automobile mechanics	29	17	7
3. Heavy Duty Mechanics	30	12	7
4. Welding and Fabrication	27	22	10
5. Carpentry and Joinry	25	16	6
6. Masonry and Concrete Work	21	18	1
7. Electrician Maintenance and Repair	26	—	—
8. Plumbing	30	—	—
9. Air Conditioning and Refrigeration Mechanics	26	25	6

Sources: Training statistics – 1982/84, op. cit., derived from p. 41.

students who join the program is increasing each year. Third-year students number only 51, whereas in the second year their number increased to 135 and reached 240 trainees in the first year. No females are recruited in this program.

Training in the Banking Sector

As the banking activities flourished in recent years, a specific council for vocational training in the banking sector was established by the High Council for Vocational Training in 1980. The specific council is headed by the chairman of Bahrain Monetary Institute and has eight members representing all the banking sector. The main objective for the council is to set policies and programs for trainee bank employees by offering them different courses related to management and banking activities. The first trainees program was established in 1983, when 876 trainees joined the program. Of all trainees 33% were females. Funding for the training activites is paid fully by all the existing banks in Bahrain, including off-shore banking units and investment banks. The amount of money paid is equivalent to

1% of the salaries of all employees working in the banks. At present, the banking sector is facing financial difficulties. To cope with the continuing recession, it is diversifying its activities. Offshore Bahrain Banking Units (OBUs) are striving to keep their position in balance. Some banks started reducing the number of their staff. This recent development makes expansion in the training program more risky.

Hotel and Catering Training Program

The prosperity in the last decade brought with it an expansion in the hotel industry. At present, there are 1,400 supervisory jobs in hotels all over Bahrain. In addition, there are nearly 30,000 other jobs in reception, management, room service and other related occupations. Such occupations are currently filled by foreigners.

To meet the demands of such expansion, a Center for Hotel and Catering Training was established in 1975. The main objective of the center is to train Bahrainis to acquire different skills related to catering and hotel management in order to replace foreigners working in that sector.

The center provides training in major departments of the hotel and catering sector. Such departments include production kitchens, a housekeeping unit and a language laboratory to teach students English and French. In addition, there is a residential annex including facilities for trainees from other Gulf states.

The center currently accepts high school diploma holders and offers a 2-year full-time training course leading to the Diploma in Hotel Operations. Students who have finished the intermediate level (grade nine) are also accepted to join the program.

At the beginning, few students joined the program; 25 females and 9 males, and a few more males from the Gulf states. In 1985/86 the total number of those who joined the program over the last decade reached 688; 47% were females. However, the average number of those who graduate each year accounts for only 25 people, a small number compared to the demand in the hotel industry and the expansion expected in tourism in the near future.

Programs Limited to Female Participation

Sewing workshop programs

These programs were established and funded by the Ministry of Labor and Social Affairs in 1975/76. They aimed at improving the standard of living of families by developing the skills of women in tailoring and sewing in order to assist them in learning a lucrative craft and securing a supplementary income. So far, eight workshops have been established in different areas all over Bahrain. Besides receiving training in tailoring and sewing over a 9-month period, the trainees receive 16 sessions on family affairs, home economics and nutrition. Ninety-six women joined the program when it was first established. By 1984/85, the total number of trainees reached 3,793 females: 71% (2692) finished the program and the rest (29%) dropped-out. They listed difficulty in transportation as a major factor for leaving the program.

Another program for sewing and tailoring was established in 1973 by the Red Crescent Society. From this program, 434 females have graduated over the last 12 years.

A third program for teaching sewing and crafts was established in 1975 by the Mother and Child Welfare Society in 1975. By 1986, 510 females had graduated from the center.

Productive families program

The program was established by the Ministry of Labor and Social Affairs, to raise the living standards of limited income families. It also aims to encourage and maintain local industries that make pottery, palm leaf products, floor mats, table mats and traditional dresses. Families who joined the program work in their homes. The finished products are marketed by the Ministry of Labor and Social Affairs through permanent exhibitions in community centers and various shops. The Ministry buys the products and re-sells them, after adding 10% to the original price. Each family gets an average monthly income equivalent to $100–120. The Ministry of Labor and Social Affairs uses the income from the sale of these purchases for further expansion. The number of those who joined the program has increased slightly over the last 8 years: 114 participants joined the program in 1978, and by

1984, the total number of participants who had joined the program had reached 191.

Hair styling training center

The Red Crescent Society opened a small training center in 1979 to train females in hair styling. Since its establishment in 1979 until 1985, 235 females joined the program. After 9 months of training, 75% of them graduated. The Society tried, successfully, to find jobs in various hairdressing salons for those who had finished training.

Goals, Objectives and Criteria

In order that training may contribute fully and effectively to ensuring that women will enjoy equal opportunities in employment, training policies should be designed on two levels: the first one should aim at women's access to training and retraining in all sectors and occupations and at all levels of skill and responsibility. The second one should be focused on programs directed at females with little or no access to education, such as the Productive Family Program, which is limited to females living in villages and working in their own homes. This program and other similar programs would help females who come from a traditional background that restricts them from working with men. Those females should be given a chance to upgrade their standard of living.

However, training programs in general, whether designed for both sexes or limited to females, should provide better and broader training so that women can acquire a stronger skills base; they should make women more productive in their work and better equipped to deal with changes.

The following goals should be implemented in order to achieve a better training program:

(a) To maintain, extend, and improve existing programs of vocational training.
(b) To develop new programs of vocational training.
(c) To provide combinations of education and employment so that persons of all ages may have ready access to vocational learning or retraining.

(d) To satisfy current and future manpower requirements.

The following objectives are of particular importance to females:

(a) To integrate women into the mainstream of training systems and programs.
(b) To increase women's participation in training for a wider range of occupations and for a higher level of skill and responsibility.
(c) To train unskilled women in skills that enable them to undertake economic projects which contribute additional income.

Whereas no single criterion is to be used in determining a program's potential success, the following points are considered to be very important in measuring the likely effectiveness of the program.

(a) The number of persons who join the training program and the proportion of women among them.
(b) The number of women who join the labor force after finishing their training.
(c) The quality of professional staff appointed to carry out the program.
(d) The cost of the training program and ways to minimize it while improving the program's quality.

Alternatives

The promotion of employment opportunities for both sexes is directly related to their skill levels. Thus, increasing the efficiency and effectiveness of training programs is essential in order to develop men and women's capabilities and skills. What is needed is more effective planning to meet the demands for the expansion and improvement of current programs. Such increased emphasis on planning for vocational training arises from several factors: limited resources, increased demands to improve existing programs and to develop new programs and demands for increased involvement in the decision-making process.

One way of judging the impact of a vocational program is by relating its performance to its stated objective. There is a close correlation between non-formal education and the creation of skills and jobs. However, with the current recession and its impact on the economy, some programs do not need massive expansion; indeed, some even need to be minimized and to focus on improving quality. The risk of oversaturating local demand with specific skills can be seen in the case of the sewing and tailoring program; this program was limited to the female population and conducted by the Ministry of Labor and Social Affairs. Thousands of females who 'graduated' from the program cannot find jobs in the local market.

There is only one option available under the present economic circumstances: expansion and improvement of the quality of current programs.

TRAINING PLAN FOR 10,000 BAHRAINIS

It has been more than 5 years since the plan was implemented; yet, most of its objectives have not been fulfilled. The plan's main goal – the training of 10,000 Bahrainis in a period of 10 years – has not been reached. Instead, an average of nearly 250 persons are trained each year, a figure that accounts for only 20% of the announced goal of 1,000 to 1,250 trained persons each year. Such results require that the contents of the program as a whole be reviewed to find out what would be most appropriate for further development. It is also of great importance to have a follow-up and an evaluation of the program each year to avoid further setbacks.

An assessment of the excessive drop-out and failure rate, which averaged 57% in 1982, is required. Special attention should be paid to female drop-outs because of the difficulty they faced in attending evening classes. However, most female participants are enrolled in Polytechnic School, where the majority study typing and the English language. These women have little access to middle level management and supervision. They are not encouraged and have no access to study such professions as engineering and management. In 1982/83, 15 females graduated from the engineering section, but they were not able to find employment anywhere in the private sector. In the same year, 90 females who graduated in bookkeeping, accounting and secretarial work failed to find jobs. Furthermore, the office of unemployed at the Ministry of Labor and Social Affairs was not able to find them jobs. Another main factor that led trainees to be discouraged from joining the program was the employers' refusal to let the trainees be released from work one day a week. Instead, they asked trainees to join evening classes so that work would not be interrupted. Females, in particular, found it more difficult to join evening classes because of family obligation.

APPRENTICESHIP TRAINING PROGRAM

This program is a direct response to employers' needs. It combines 'on-the-job' training with formal workshop instructions on a day-release basis. The Vocational Training Center at Isa town established particular courses in accordance with the demand for such training by employers. Although the program is highly dependent on employer awareness, it is considered very flexible and responsive.

Apprentices do not include females. There is an explicit policy by employers to discriminate against females in holding jobs that are considered 'men's jobs'; these include electrical work, mechanics, carpentry and plumbing (see Table 6.7). Females would be able to break social barriers gradually and join such jobs if the government passed legislation against such discrimination.

TRAINING IN THE BANKING SECTOR

The banking sector is considered the hardest hit by the recent recession. Many banks, in their efforts to cope with the shrinking market, caused mainly by the drop in oil prices, are considering many procedures to limit their costs. One such procedure is to cut down on staff. Thus, expansion in the banking training program is not advisable.

HOTELS AND CATERING TRAINING PROGRAM

The hotel business is a new booming sector in Bahrain, dominated by foreigners who work in various related jobs as managers, directors, waiters, cooks and clerks. The Hotel and

Catering Training Center, which was established to train nationals to work in hotels and catering, is a small institution that cannot cope with the demand for trained personnel. It is not so well-equipped with qualified staff and modern appliances. Classes are few and cannot absorb a larger number of students. The number of students enrolled in the program is very few compared to the number of jobs filled by foreigners working in that sector. Students, especially females, need to be encourged to join the program by being provided with incentives including better pay and promotion in their jobs.

In order to make the program more successful, two steps should be taken into consideration:

1. *An expansion of the program*: As mentioned earlier, the demand for personnel and staff far exceeds supply. The average number of graduates from the program each year is only 25. At the same time, there are 1,400 supervisory jobs in different hotels in Bahrain; this is in addition to nearly 30,000 other jobs in related occupations filled by foreigners. In order to overcome such a shortage, an expansion in the program as a whole is needed. The Training Center needs to be supplied with modern equipment and qualified staff. Additional classes should be established, and some graduates from the Center need to be sent abroad to receive higher training in different hotel catering institutions.
2. *More attention to recruitment of females* Although the percentage of females is considered relatively high in the program as a whole (47%), the number of those who join the program for both sexes is very low. Cultural factors keep females from seeking jobs in this sector. Such factors include the following:

   (a) Females are discriminated against in promotion to managerial positions.
   (b) It is culturally undesirable for a female to work as a waitress serving alcoholic beverages to customers. An increasing number of hotel occupants come from neighboring Gulf states, which makes it even more unacceptable for Bahraini females to hold such jobs.
   (c) It is very difficult for females to work night shifts and

leave their homes at night. This makes hotel managers reluctant to hire them.

However, females can handle jobs not conflicting with their culture or family life. They can work as receptionists, telephone operators, supervisors, managers, clerical workers and secretaries. Furthermore, they should be given priority to work during the day, a step that might encourage a large number of them to join this sector.

PROGRAMS LIMITED TO FEMALE PARTICIPANTS

Sewing workshop programs

In spite of the increasing number of females who have joined the program, the drop-out rate is fairly high. Of the 3,793 trainees who have joined the program over the last 10 years, only 2,622 have finished the program. This brings the drop-out rate to 29%. The high drop-out rate is primarily due to difficulty in transportation and a lack of sufficient financial support for the program. Another fact that has added to the drop-out rate is that some young females, mostly from villages, joined the program to be prepared for marriage. They leave after acquiring the training they consider adequate for married life.

However, the program is not considered successful because those who graduated from the program could not find jobs. Employers prefer to import foreign tailors rather than hire Bahraini females. They claim that foreign tailors are more efficient and cost less than local tailors. The 1981 census revealed that the number of tailors and dressmakers reached 2,445; Bahrainis, including both sexes, account for only 171 and Bahraini females account for 72 or 3% of the total.[8] Therefore, expansion of the program is not advisable at present until a solution is found for the large number of females who have graduated from the program and have not been able to find jobs. The following steps are recommended to improve the program outcome in general and to link it to the labor market demand in particular:

1. Limiting the number of visas for foreign tailors.
2. Passing legislation that obliges employers to recruit a

percentage of those who graduated from the program.
3. Recruiting more qualified staff, and making the training period longer.

Productive families program

The type of handicraft produced by workers in this program is vanishing as a job craft, but in an effort to preserve it as a folk industry, the Ministry of Labor and Social Affairs supports it by paying the workers monthly allowances. This kind of craft, which is found in most villages, depends on palm tree leaves and is mainly seen as an expected activity for females. Most of the trainees in the program are illiterate females who inherited the profession from their mothers. In order to improve the quality and productivity, the following is recommended:

1. Recruiting more staff to improve the training of the families and to make them more creative in designing the handicrafts.
2. Encouraging participants to join literacy classes in order to create more awareness among them.

Hair styling program

This program is relatively small. Suggestions to improve it include increasing the budget in order to hire well-trained staff and to furnish the center with better equipment.

Conclusion

Major expansions in the technical and vocational training system are required to overcome skill shortages. Adequate attention should be given to the training of school drop-outs and unemployed youth. Prime candidates for training will be found among the larger number of women who are entering and re-entering the labor force. In addition to their greater numbers in the total population, their participation in the labor force (full-time and part-time) should increase as well. Efforts to serve women and encourage non-stereotypical career choices should be concentrated on those re-entering the labor market.

The government should develop measures for expanding training opportunities for women and should encourage them to enter a broader range of occupations. One such approach is to encourage women to train or retrain in occupations where they are underrepresented; to create additional training places for women in present occupations, to establish quotas for women in training and apprenticeship courses, to make entry requirements more flexible, and to provide pre-training courses to enable women to make up for deficiences in their education.

Many females find evening classes very difficult to attend because of family obligations and social norms that keep women confined to their homes in the evenings. This problem requires an intervention by the government in the form of legislation that would oblige employers to release the trainees to join training sessions on a regular basis. The government should also penalize employers who refuse to do this.

The program would be improved if those who graduated found jobs. This would be possible if there were legislation that obliged employers to hire a certain percentage of nationals for their staff, as is the case in other Gulf states. The government of Bahrain is reluctant to do this, fearing that foreign companies would move to neighboring Dubai in the United Arab Emirates, where there are no restrictions on hiring foreign workers.

Policy decisions regarding vocational training will be more effective if efficient data on manpower shortages is available. Such data can be acquired from the following resources:

(a) The Isa Town Vocational Training Center, which was established in 1979, could indicate areas where there are a shortage of skills, as it was established to meet such a shortfall.

(b) The employment office at the Ministry of Labor and Social Affairs is another useful source of data regarding vacancies and salary levels by which manpower shortages may be identified. The importance of vacancy data is that it covers a broader range of employers and occupational requirements than vocational training data.[9]

Some important administrative and financial issues need to be implemented in order to improve the programs' outcome. These are discussed below.

HIGH COUNCIL FOR VOCATIONAL TRAINING

This council was established in 1975 to represent employers, employees and the government. In addition to those groups, the council should include vocational training experts as advisers. Those experts would make recommendations on current job needs and the relevance of the programs being offered. Experts would also assist the council with the development of its annual application to the government submitted for approval and financial support. Furthermore, there must be an appropriate representation of both sexes. For example, those who are in charge of programs limited to females should join the council to help determine the needs of training programs and to advise the council members in determining policies that encourage more women to join the program.

STAFF

The existing vocational training center (Isa Town) cannot supply the extensive manpower demands with its limited capacity. The main causes that made the center fail to meet such demands were lack of proper funding and the inability to recruit qualified staff. However, hiring competent technical staff requires a substantial financial investment. In addition, staff should be evaluated by such criteria as: their ability to plan and conduct instruction, their organization and control of class, their rapport with students and other staff members and their willingness to accept constructive criticism and to try to improve performance. The quality of staff performances should also be measured by: the observation of student participation and performance, the degree of success achieved by students when employed and the evaluation report of supervisor and principal.[10]

Vocational education program planning is a continuous process. The staff should be involved in planning. The results of staff involvement in the planning process are constructive: professional staff are able to produce accurate data and information and their involvement would help to verify the completeness and appropriateness of program elements. Furthermore, since they will be the implementers of the plan, the staff must verify the plan elements in terms of day-to-day practice in the classroom.

COST

Vocational education usually costs more per student contact hour than academic education. Without adequate funds to carry out planning process, the usefulness of the programs will be greatly reduced.

Finding out what resources are available is very important. At present, the levy system is used to cover the expense of all vocational training programs in Bahrain, and so private companies participate in training costs. As mentioned previously, the out put of formal education is not sufficiently related to the needs of employers. This fact has led the government to seek a greater share of training costs from employers, but some employers were reluctant to assure a larger financial role, fearing that those in-company trainees will leave their jobs for better-paid ones. Consequently, some companies have cut back on this form of training. The present levy system in Bahrain excludes large and powerful companies from participating in this system. This tends to limit the programs to cover only small companies. In 1979/80 when the levy system was founded, only 33 establishments were paying levy which totaled nearly $3 m for the first 2 years. In 1984 the total levey received from 56 establishments increased to nearly $3.8 m.[11]

The government should address this problem by implementing a levy system in which all employers contribute through a compulsory levy to a training fund. Companies conducting on-the-job training will be reimbursed for training costs out of this fund. This system guarantees that if those who conduct training lose their trainees they will be losing them to enterprises that have shared part of the training cost. The levy system, if applied properly, would help to finance training programs.

Although these are very modest proposals, it would be a step in the right direction because there would then be a structure and a policy for vocational training. If everything goes well and if Bahrain carries out all the proposed programs and legislation, circumstances will require a much bigger effort in creating and increasing vocational training programs.

Notes

1. *Equal Opportunity and Equal Treatment for Men and Women in Employment*, report, 11V, International Labor Conference 71st Session 1985, ILO, Geneva, 1985, p. 29.
2. Nadia Youssef, 'Education and Female Modernism in the Muslim World', *Journal of International Affairs*, vol. 30, no. 2, 1976–77, p. 207.
3. *Equal Opportunity and Equal Treatment for Men and Women in Employment*, report 11V, International Labor Conference 71st Session, ILO, Geneva, 1985, p. 30.
4. Ismael Serageldin, James Socknat, Stace Birks, Bob Li, Clive Sinclair, *Manpower and International Labor Migration in the Middle East and North Africa*, Oxford, 1983, Table 4-6, p. 33.
5. *Statistical Abstracts/1984*, Council of Ministers, Central Statistics Organization, Bahrain, 1985, p. 116.
6. Sami Zuraiqat, *Khuttat Tadreeb Ashrat Ala-ph Bahraini fi Santeha al-thalitha: ardh wa teqyeem*, (Training plan for 10,000 Bahraini in its third year: an assessment), Bahrain, 1983 (Arabic), p. 1.
7. Jassem Abu-Suhail, *Taqyeem khutat tadreeb ashrat ala-ph Bahraini*, (evaluation of training plan for 10,000 Bahraini), The Arabic Planning Institute. Kuwait, 1982, (Arabic), p. 64.
8. *Bahrain Census of Population and Housing-1981*, Bahrain 1982, p. 81.
9. Ian Seccombe, *International Labor Migration and Skill Scarcity in the hashimite Kingdom of Jordan*, ILO, Geneva 1983, p. 20.
10. William Bently, *Administering the Successful Vocational Education, a Guide for Administrators*, 1978, p. 84.
11. *Training Statistics, 1982–1984*, Ministry of Labor and Social Affairs, Bahrain, 1985, p. 7.

Chapter Seven

Future Directions

The heavy reliance upon foreign labor in Bahrain is related to the boom of the post-oil economic infrastructure, which grew dramatically after 1973. The governments of Bahrain and of the other Gulf states responded to the manpower shortage by importing more foreign workers in large numbers until their number reached an alarming figure. Foreign workers constituted 81,497 or 55.8% of the total workforce in 1981 and nearly one-third of the entire population of Bahrain, counting spouses and dependents.

The government of Bahrain is reluctant to formulate clear migration policies. It fears that foreign workers will become an organized power to such an extent that they will ask for better living conditions and higher salaries. To limit such a threat, the government started adopting different policies. One policy was to diversify foreign labor nationalities in order to prevent one group from becoming a strong power.

National manpower formed 44.2% of the total labor force (8.3% females and 35.9% males) in 1981. Inadequacy in the educational system and the lack of efficient training programs are seen as major factors contributing to the decline in national manpower through the substitution of foreign labor.

What adds to the problem is the demographic structure of the population, which makes overall male participation relatively low. Thus, the only alternative that would help in increasing the proportion of the national labor force would be to employ more female nationals. However, many cultural, social and religious barriers keep females from joining the labor force. In addition, the low level of the females' education and training, and the inefficiency in quality and quantity of child-care services play an important part in keeping females and young mothers from joining the labor force.

With the decrease in oil revenues in early 1980s, the foreign labor problems became more critical: many of the unskilled workers are being sent back to their home countries or their contracts are not being renewed, but the skilled foreign laborers will be even more needed in most jobs that required the specializations, which most indigenous workers lacked. Thus, Bahrain will be more dependent on such skilled workers for future development projects and for the maintenance of current projects.

It is proposed then, that female nationals should be encouraged to join the labor force. Family policy, therefore, should be used as an instrument to enhance female integration into the labor market. This means that a combination of labor market policy with family policy should aim at stimulating women to enter the labor force and to achieve more equality between the sexes. Such policy will present women with a new sense of economic independence, which is vital to changing their traditional self-image. Furthermore, their financial status will be improved and they will play a greater role in the development process that is taking place in Bahrain and in the Gulf region at present.

Integrating more women in the labor force would offer a partial solution to labor market demands and would limit the foreign labor threat. At the same time, this would improve the situation of women in particular and the society as a whole in general. It is recommended, then, that a comprehensive policy must focus on the labor market policy and must facilitate women's participation in the labor force by means of a package consisting of the following legislation and programs:

(a) Establishing more day-care facilities.
(b) Eradicating the illiteracy of women and issuing a law for compulsory education.
(c) Increasing the proportion of females in current vocational training programs.
(d) Issuing a progressive family law.

Implementation of the Proposed Legislation and Programs

The proposed package of legislation and programs is designed to increase women's participation in the labor force. This policy needs to be planned carefully without causing any harm to the family. However, implementing such programs would be a task of great difficulty and the way of implementation might lead to the failure or to a long postponement of the programs. This leads us to discuss the implementation process in Bahrain and in other developing countries in more detail.

Implementation is defined as the phase in which the plan of action is translated into action. The task of implementation is defined as the establishment of a link that allows the goals of policies to be realized as outcomes of governmental activities.[1] A failure of any program happens when implementation becomes separated from policy.[2]

In the Third World countries, many factors can contribute to the weakening of any government policy: the lack of qualified personnel, insufficient direction and control from political leaders and opposition to the policy itself and corruption. For successful implementation, Quick recommends that the goals of public programs must be agreed upon by both political and administrative officials at all levels in the government hierarchy.[3] In addition, other factors intervene between the statement of policy goals and their actual achievement in the society. These are such factors as the availability of sufficient resources, the commitment of officials and the political leverage of opponents of the policy.

Implementation, even when successful, involves far more than the mechanical translation of goals into routine procedures; it involves fundamental questions about conflict, decision making and the population who are served by the programs.

As for Bahrain and the Gulf region in general, the administrative structure is still inefficient. This inefficiency became more clear in the last decade: the increase in public projects and services required a more advanced administrative body to implement these programs. This had led to a failure in keeping up with the development programs. At the same time, the government's policy of providing jobs to nationals regardless of their qualifications has led to an enormous expansion of the administration, duplication of duties and a conflict of responsibilities. The result has been the emergence of what has been termed 'beduinocracy',[4] in which the choice and promotion of officials depend mainly on social factors and nepotism rather than on merits. This has led to low productivity and a weak incentive system and a failure in implementing development projects. To avoid such a failure for the proposed programs, some administrative issues will be discussed in the following paragraphs:

The first program deals with child-care services in Bahrain (Chapter Four). Demands for such programs are increasing, mostly from mothers who wish to work outside the home. The needs for adequate day-care facilities, nurseries and kindergartens will increase even more over the next few years. However, the main problem that faces the implementation of this program will be the conflicting administrative roles. Child-care services in Bahrain are controlled by three governmental bodies (the Ministries of Education, Labor and Social Affairs and the High Council for Youth and Sports). Such a structural arrangement makes implementing the program more difficult. What adds to the problem is the exclusion of the Ministry of Health from taking any positive role in policy formulation concerning child-care services. The fragmentation of administrative roles would weaken the implementation process and lead to program failure. Therefore, integrating the four administrative bodies into one committee would make the implementation process much easier. In addition, this committee would take the responsibility of formulating the child-care policy, coordinating the four governmental bodies, assessing and evaluating different child care programs and recommending steps to be taken for future planning.

The second program was on education and female employment (Chapter Five). Different statistics and studies on Bahrain and on the Middle East in general have demonstrated a close relationship between the increased rates of women's participation in the labor force and their access to education: the higher the level of education, the greater the women's employability. At the same time, statistics indicate that illiterate females aged 10–44 years constituted 80% (20,506) of all illiterate persons of that age group. Such a high female illiteracy rate limits the participation of women in the labor force.

Planning a literacy program requires a unified plan for compulsory education that goes hand in hand with the 5-year-plan that is in effect in Bahrain at present. Besides issuing legislation for compulsory education, there should be stress placed on iniating different measures which would make the 5-year-plan more successful, such measures as: the use of mass media, the training of the staff for literacy programs, the full participation of women's associations and providing funds for the plan.

Programs, similar to the proposed literacy program, that are designed to achieve long-range objectives, may be more difficult to implement than those whose advantages are immediately apparent to the beneficiaries therefore, providing a large amount of money to implement these long-range programs would be a difficult task.

The third proposed program of providing vocational training for females (Chapter Six), deals with education and training outside the formal educational structure. It is considered an important part of the non-formal educational system that would help females join the labor market. The success of this program does not rely mainly on administrative or cost issues as is the case with the previous programs. The problem would be rather one of a cultural background. Females would find it very difficult to break the social barriers and hold such jobs considered to be 'men's jobs' as working as an electrical worker, mechanic, or carpenter – or to hold jobs in the booming tourist sector in which the workers have to deal with tourists coming mainly from the neighboring Gulf states. Therefore, besides passing legislation against such job discrimination, the government should create more awareness within the community in order to encourage men and women to play equal roles in society and in the economy as well.

The last proposed legislation is the issuing of a progressive family law (Chapter Three). The present political system will not be able to pass such legislation. The Islamic principles of Shri'a (religious code) governing women and the family as a whole are playing an essential role in strengthening the political system, which is based mainly on tribal rule and the preservation of the status quo; these principles are strengthening the traditional elite and the religious institution. The secularization of personal laws through the establishment of a civil code contradicts what the tribal system stands for. Therefore, the study of public policy must include the study of the political system itself and of the distribution of effective power within it, if the possibility for the implementation of the proposed programs and legislation is to be assessed. It is important to attempt to understand, as fully as possible, what factors might lead to the program's failure and what conditions might lead to more successful performance in the future.

Political Modernization in Bahrain

Bahrain, like all the Gulf states, is a tribal society government by a ruling family that only recently started to encourage a degree of popular participation. This experiment, which started in 1973, lasted for 2 years but ended in 1975.

The tribal rule in Bahrain has realized that any future expansion of popular participation in government will result in contraction of the authority of the ruling family.[5] In other words, the perception is that public representation and the standardization of laws eventually destroys the exclusiveness and non-assimilative character of the tribal groups and the collective control of action and behavior. Giving the right to women of education and of employment undermines the authority of the religiously oriented people who support the existing regimes. Any such concessions will eventually work against the tribal control of government and the monopoly of power.[6]

In the following paragraphs, the theory of modernization will be presented and applied to the political system in Bahrain and the Gulf region in general to assess the modernization process that is taking place there:

The origin of the modernization theory may be traced to the response of American social scientists to the international setting of the post-World War II era. During the two decades after the war, American social scientists paid more attention to the problems of economic development, political stability and social and cultural change in the Third World societies of Asia, Africa and Latin America. Also, social scientists assumed that the institutions and values of American society represented an appropriate model to be adopted by developing countries. The idea of modernization appealed to American policy-makers so much that development and modernization came to be viewed as long-range solutions to the threats of instability and Communism in the Third World.[7]

The main characteristics that were assigned by early writers to the modernization process will be summarized in the following paragraphs. Modernization is a revolutionary process to the extent of the changes it brings about in traditional society; at the same time, it is evolutionary because of the amount of time required to bring about these changes. Modernization also is a phased process; societies begin in the traditional stage and end in the modern stage. It is also an irreversible process; a society that has reached a certain level of urbanization, literacy and industrialization in one decade will not decline to substantially lower levels in the next decade. It is also a progressive process: the cost of the pains in its early phases, is great, but the achievement of modern, social, political and economic order is worth it.[8]

By the late 1960s, some theorists started to identify some of the difficulties of modernization theory. The criticism that these analysts made of the traditional theory of modernization focused on the meaning and usefulness of the concepts of modernity and tradition, the relationship between modernity and tradition and the ambiguities in the concept of modernization itself. However, many modernization theorists pointed out that traditional societies are not static. The view that tradition and innovation are necessarily in conflict has begun to seem to be an unrealistic one. Moreover, the assertion that modernization in one sphere will necessarily produce compatible changes in other spheres seems unrealistic also; as an example, modernizing the military sector cannot bring changes in other sectors of society. Thus selective modernization may only strengthen traditional institutions and values. The rapid social change in one sphere may serve only to inhibit changes in others. Furthermore, the distinction between modernization and modernity must be emphasized. Many such attributes of modernization as widespread literacy or modern medicine have appeared or have been adopted, but in isolation from the other attributes of modern society. Therefore, modernization in some spheres of life may occur without resulting in modernity.[9] This is similar to the kind of modernization that has been undertaken in Bahrain and in the Gulf states, where rapid development occurred in the educational, industrial, military and financial sectors, whereas development in the politial sector was ignored.

However, some critics support the revisionist option of modernization theory. Others say that a radical solution be reached that would reject the whole concept of modernization and look for an alternative. Such criticism made it possible for a 'neo-Marxist' school of development theory to emerge. This school started in the late 1960s in Latin America, and was represented, for many, by Andre Gunder Frank. The new development theory, which is widely known as the dependency theory, stresses the interconnectedness of development, of traditional and modern, and of everything in general; it sees many conflicts and clashes of interest in the development process, both between nations and between social forces within under-developed countries. It sees development as a revolutionary break rather than as a continuing evolution from the present; and it advocates socialism.[10]

Galtung emphasizes the concept of 'Center' and 'Periphery' as one central theme of the dependency theory. The impact of rich upon poor nations can be understood if the global political economy is viewed as the relationship between a 'Center' (the developed countries) and a 'Periphery' (the less developed countries), each of which is further subdivided into its own 'Center' (the governing elite) and 'Periphery' (groups without much power or wealth). The power is not exercised directly, through the offer of benefits or threat of sanctions by the Center to a peripheral nation, rather, the power is exercised through collaborating elites in the subordinate country.[11] Thus, these elites in developing countries are the principal agents in transmitting foreign influence to the national scene. The more fully private direct investment dominates the economic life of a developing country, the position of these elites will be stronger and marginalization of the rest of the population will be greater. In sum, almost all dependency theorists agree that extensive and highly concentrated ties between developing countries and developed countries in areas of trade, aid, investment, debt, higher education and arms transfer tend to result in control by the elites of the Periphery. These elites can be expected to prevent meaningful distribution of social welfare policies that might threaten their dominance at home, to devote considerable attention to expand their coercive apparatus and in general, to follow a development strategy that meets their own needs but is inappropriate to the needs of non-elites of their countries. The ultimate result of a distorted development pattern of this sort is that non-elites are drawn into a set of structural relationships in which their relative position can only deteriorate.[12]

Critics of the dependency theory claim that this theory is still at an early stage of development, a theory with various gaps that need to be filled up and ambiguities to be resolved. Smith argues that dependency theory in general overestimates the power of international system in the affairs of developing countries. He asserts that dependency theory has systematically underestimated the real influence of the developing countries over their own affairs, and that native political forces played a fairly powerful role in the colonies even when they failed to control top political positions of the state. Smith agrees that dependency theory is correct when it maintains that the power of developed countries influences the course of economic, social and political development in developing countries. However, it is essential that the strength and independence of local factors should not be forgotten.[13]

Critics of the dependency theory also claim that it is difficult to draw a line between dependence and non-dependence. It seems to be more sensible to think in terms of scale and not of the absolute presence or absence of dependence. It is true that developing countries depend for their technology on advanced countries, and that this technology is, in some ways, inappropriate to the production and consumption needs of developing countries, and that it leads to social ills, misdirected science and education policies. Further, it is argued that whereas it is true that developing countries, including Bahrain and the Gulf region, exhibit some or all of these characteristics, some economies that are classified as non-dependent also show some characteristics of dependence; for example, some European countries complain just as much about the 'American challenge' as do nationals in developing countries.[14] In a world of interdependence, this means that it is a question of scale and not of the absolute presence of dependence. In other words, the difference is a matter of degree rather than of kind.

Bahrain's case confirms both modernization theory and dependency theory. Recent industrialization in Bahrain would lead to more rationalization. As a natural outcome, equality will be increased. At the same time, dependency theory could be applied partially to Bahrain; the economy is mostly controlled by multinational corporations especially in the financial and oil sectors, but the state maintains some power on the internal affairs.

Because the previous models that social scientists have devised during the last two decades to describe present and future development-processes in developing countries were of limited use when applied to Bahrain and the Gulf States, Nakhleh emphasized the need for a fresh theoretical attempt at model building in the Gulf. Nakhleh calls the new model the urban tribalism model.[15] This model is designed to represent a new reality and to anticipate future changes in this reality. The urban tribalism model is at an initial stage and in need of further research. It is a combination of traditional tribalism and modernity. Urbanization in the Gulf states has proven to be a long process, consisting mainly of one major component – the transformation of a tribal culture into a twentieth-century organization within which the Islamic principles of Shari'a (religious code) and Shura (consultation) find expression in the modern political techniques of political democracy. This model (urban tribalism), Nakhleh concludes, is a description of the emerging result of synthesizing traditional tribalism and modernization – the new Gulf community.[16] However, the political developments of the last decade that culminated in the dissolution of the National Assembly have proved that any kind of popular participation would eventually destroy tribal political regimes. In any case, it is hard to say that Bahrain could institute a democracy while the other Gulf states continue to have tribal governments.

Future Directions

Bahrain and the Gulf region have undergone drastic social and economic changes in the last few decades. But the changes in the last decade that took place after the sharp increase in oil revenues were more evident. As an example, expansion in education in the last 50 years was enormous; the number of students enrolled in schools increased from 500 boys and 100 girls in 1931 to reach a total of 87,144 (45,668 boys and 41,376 girls) in 1983/84, in both private and public sectors. This increase in education has had great consequences. In the past, higher education was limited to a small elite who controlled the highest positions in the society. With the establishment of universities and colleges for higher education in Bahrain and in the Gulf region, the outcome may become very different; this means that more highly educated people from different social levels could reach these top level positions.

The increase in oil revenues has affected other sectors as well. The development of industry in such fields as oil production, manufacturing industries, banking and finance, and even in tourism has been enormous. Furthermore, there has been a great expansion in housing that has led to the weakening of the traditional extended family and to the emergence of the nuclear one.

The growth of the population over the last 40 years has increased four times, and it is expected to reach nearly half a million in the year 1991. Moreover, nearly 54.4% of the Bahraini population is under 20 years of age. This demographic change adds to the amount of strain policy-makers in Bahrain are facing in dealing with such problems including providing this young population with adequate schooling and jobs.

The rapid improvement in health services has helped in decreasing the mortality rate and in increasing the birth rate. Thus, the raising of children becomes more expensive; instead of being an asset as in the past, chidren have become an economic burden.

In addition, foreign laborers and their dependents make up altogether one-third of the population. Foreign labor brought with it different ideas, which has affected the local people in many aspects of their lives.

More importantly, the number of females who join the labor force is increasing each year. This recent phenomenon is expected to have a great impact on family life and will lead to more equality between the sexes.

These economic and social changes, which have taken place in a short period of time, have represented new challenges to the tribal rule in Bahrain and to the Gulf region in general, and also they have revealed the failure of the political system to adapt itself to such changes.

These changes should lead us, therefore, to redefine the target of development, which means, in this case, growth plus change. Economic growth alone is never an adequate basis for the formulation of the target: society must assess its overall political and resource realities; society's performance is dependent on an image for the development which emerges. The question becomes 'what kind of a society do we wish to become, given our resources, our potentialities, and our motivation?'[17] However, a great part of anticipation of the future is affected by what we think we, ourselves, will become and of what our societies will become, since change arises with society from needs felt by the people. Sometimes economic and social changes produce discontent even though they are planned to bring about desirable changes. Such changes require modernization of the political system.

There are two prevailing concepts about the future of the Gulf: there are those who view the future with despair and argue that the oil era will soon reach an end because none of the preconditions for a comprehensive development exists: whereas, others believe that development is possible if careful planning is used to convert this sudden prosperity into real economic development, bearing in mind the inescapable fact that every barrel of oil extracted reduces the number of barrels left to be produced in the future.[18]

With the expected depletion of oil in the 1990s, the future of Bahrain will be linked entirely to the future of the Gulf states, especially Saudi Arabia. Thus, Bahrain could benefit more as the GCC develops more integration among member states. As a matter of fact, Bahrain could play an important role within the GCC states, as was the case during the British rule when Bahrain became the political center of the region; it served as the headquarters of the protectorate in the Gulf. Today, Bahrain could play a similar role with the GCC states; that is to become the financial and tourist center: having limited resources and a relatively educated population, policy-makers in Bahrain decided to develop a service economy. Bahrain already established itself as an international financial center. Even with the declining financial situation in the Gulf, Bahrain still has 175 banks, including local, foreign and off-shore banking (OBUs). The total assets of OBUs reached $60–65 b, of which 75% are US dollar assets.

Economic and trade policies will keep Bahrain as the financial center of the region. Bahrain adapted its laws so that the Gulf and foreign firms were able to get established. There is the possibility of developing a GCC stock market in Bahrain, and this would strengthen the existing market and diversify the economy, away from banking.[19] The economic unification of the GCC would profit Bahrain the most.

In addition, Bahrain is expected to become a tourist center for the Gulf region. There are many projects under construction to attract more tourists. The relative openness of the society and Bahrain's being the only state in the region that permits the sale of alcohol have made tourism flourish in recent years.

In conclusion, these results that I am predicting here indicate that both modernization and dependency theories are partially right. One cannot deny that the system worked for a long time in the past; today, the people of Bahrain and the Gulf region have outgrown this tribal system. The popular demand for political participation and democracy is increasing (modernization theory). The government was holding different groups together to be loyal mainly by money in the form of contracts, incentives, subsidies, favors and donations. With the sharp decrease in oil revenues in recent years, the political system's relations with such groups will be deteriorated. In fact, many have started speaking out more openly on public affairs, arguing that a move to modernize the political system is more urgent than ever.

However, the direction in which Bahrain and the Gulf states will move certainly will not be shaped by the people of the Gulf alone (dependency theory) because the future of oil, and with it the authority system, is tied economically and politically to the larger industrial world.[20]

As we have seen, there is a modernization theory that predicts and explains what is going on in Bahrain and the Gulf region in general. We also gained a considerable insight from dependency theory: of no small importance the world influence will affect the GCC and Bahrain. Finally we nave noted that reforms in family law are significant. There is no basis in political theory for predicting how these interacting forces will eventually interact together to shape Bahrain's future. Their interaction, however, will create a context in which the recommendations developed in this study will prove to be feasible or completely unrealistic.

Notes

1. Merilee Grindle (Ed.), *Politics and Policy Implementation in the Third World* (Princeton University Press, 1980) p. 6.
2. J. L. Pressman and A. Wildavsky, *Implementation* Berkeley, Los Angeles: University of California Press, London, 1973, p. 143.
3. Stephen A. Quick, 'The Paradox of Plurality: Ideological Program Implementation in Zambia', in Grindle, M. (Ed.), op. cit., p. 41.
4. M. Rumaihi, *Beyond Oil: Unity and Development in the Gulf*, London: Al-Saqi Books, 1986, p. 48.
5. Emile Nakhleh, *Bahrain*, Mass.: Lexington Books, 1976, p. 11.
6. Foad Khuri, *Tribe and State in Bahrain: the Transformation of Social and Political Authority in an Arab State*, Chicago University Press, 1980, p. 244.
7. Dean C. Tipps, 'Modernization Theory and the Comparative Study of Society: A Critical Perspective', *Comparative Studies in Society and History*, 15 (2) 1973 p. 208.
8. Samuel P. Huntingdon, 'The Change to Change: Modernization, Development and Politics', *Comparative Politics*, vol. 3, 1971, p. 289.
9. Reinhard Bendix, 'Tradition and Modernity Reconsidered', *Comparative Studies in Society and History*, 9, 3, 1967, p. 329.
10. Aiden Foster-Carter, 'From Rostow to Gunder Frank: Conflicting Paradigms in the Analysis of Underdevelopment', *World Development*, vol. 4, no. 3, (Mar. 1976) p. 174.
11. Vincent A. Mahler, *Dependency Approaches to International Political Economy: A Cross National Study*, New York: Columbia University Press, 1980, p. 53.
12. Ibid., p. 68.
13. Tony Smith, 'The Underdevelopment of Development Literature: the Case of Dependency Theory', *World Politics*, vol. XXXI, no. 1 (Oct. 1978) pp. 261 and 283.
14. Sanjaya Lall, 'Is 'Dependence' a Useful Concept in Analysing Under-Development', *World Development*, vol. 3, 11–12 (1975) p. 803.
15. Emile Nakhleh, op. cit., p. 167.
16. Ibid., p. 167.
17. Alfred Khan, *Studies in Social Policy and Planning*, New York: Russell Sage Foundation, 1969, p. 308.
18. M. G. Rumaihi, *Beyond Oil: Unity and Development in the Gulf*, London: Al-Saqi Books, 1986, pp. 38–9.
19. Jean-Francois Seznec, *The Financial Markets of the Arabian Gulf: Bahrain, Kuwait, Saudi Arabia* (forthcoming), London: Croom Helm, 1987, p. 238.
20. Foad Khuri, op. cit., p. 247.

Bibliography

Abhath wa Dirasat Nadwat Al-Istikhdam al-Amthal lil-Quwa Al-Amila Al-Wataneyyah (Research and studies of the seminar held in Muscat, Oman, 26–29 Nov. 1984), Maktab Al-Mutaba's, Oman, 1984 (Arabic).

Abu Nasr, Julinda, Koury, Nabil F. and Azzam, Henry T. (Ed.), *Women, Employment and Development in the Arab World*. Berlin, New York and Amsterdam: Mouton Publishers, 1985.

Abu-Saud, Abeer, *Qatari Women, Past and Present*, Harlow, Essex: Longman, 1984.

Abu-suhail, Jassem. *Taqyeem khuttat tadreeb ashrat ala-ph Bahraini* (Evaluation of training plan for 10,000 Bahraini), Kuwait: The Arab Planning Institute, 1982 (Arabic).

Ahmad, Muhammed Abbas, *Mudhakkara raqum arba'a bisha'ni khutta litadribel-Amileen* (report No. 4 regarding a plan to train literacy workers), Bahrain, Feb., 1983 (Arabic).

Ahmad, M. A., Al-Khalifa, M. F. and Farrag, M. *Baramej mahwel-ummeyah wata'leemel-kibar bedowlatel-Bahrain* (Programs of eradicating literacy and adult education in Bahrain 1984/85, Bahrain, 1984 (Arabic).

Ahmad, M. A., Alkhalifa, M. F. and Darrah, A. *Waqi' Albaramej almutatawerah lemahwel-ummeyah wta'leem alkibar bel-Bahrain* (Programs for adult education in Bahrain, 1983 (Arabic).

Al-Alawi, Hashim, *Dirasah watalkhees: Addowrah attadribeyah, allati qama bedowalel-khaleej bedowlatel – Bahrain men tareekh insha-ih 1977 hatta nehayat 1984* (A study and summary of the training sessions held in the Literacy Training Center for the Gulf states in Bahrain from 1977–84), Bahrain, 1984 (Arabic).

Al-Awdha' Al-Iqtisadeyyah Wal-Ijtima'eyyah Lil-Mar'a Al-Bahraineyyah, dirash maydaneyyah (Social and economic conditions of women in Bahrain), a field study, Ministry of Labor and Social Affairs, Economic Commission for Western Asia (ECWA), and the Institute for Research, Beirut, Bahrain, 1985 (Arabic).

Al-Essa, Shamlan, Y. *The manpower problem in Kuwait*, London and

New York: Kegan Paul International, 1981.

Al-Jabi, Ghada, *Almushkilat-allati ta'taredh musharakatel-mar'a fi nashat mahwel-ummeyah waqterahel-hulul allati tusa-id ala tousi' musharakatiha* (Problems facing the participatin of women in literacy programs and suggesting solutions that help in more participation), paper presented to the seminar held in Damscus, Syria, 6–10 Jan. 1985, on the role of women's leaders in adapting successful measures in adult education, 1985 (Arabic).

Al-Kazi, Lubna A., *The Dilemma of Ultra-rapid Development: The Reliance on Migrant Labour in the Oil Rich Gulf States* (Dissertation), University of Texas at Austin, 1983.

Al-Kazi, Lubna, A. *The Impact of Education on Women's Economic Participation: A Case Study of Kuwaiti Women*, Paper presented to the Regional Planning Conference for Arab Women, Nicosia, Cyprus, 24–29 June 1985. Organized by the Institute of Women's Studies in the Arab World, Beirut, Lebanon, 1985.

Al-Khameery, Hissa, *Taqreer-an mahwel-ummeyah bidowlatel Bahrain* (A report on adult education regarding women in Bahrain), seminar held in Baghdad, Iraq, from 3–8 Dec. 1977 (Arabic).

Al-Misnad, Shaikha, *The Development of Modern Education in the Gulf*, London: Ithaca Press, 1985.

Al-Mustaqbal Al-Arabi, vol. 4, no. 50 (Apr. 1983).

Al-Yamamah, vol. 32 (791), (22 Feb. 1984) pp. 74–8. (Arabic)

American Arab Affairs, no. 7 (Winter 1983–84), Washington, D.C.: American–Arab Affairs Council.

Amin, Sayed Hassan, *Political and Strategic Issues in the Gulf*, Royston Limited, England, 1984.

Anderson, Karl, *With the Same Right as Other: About Migrants on the Swedish Labor Market*, in *Labor Market Reforms in Sweden* (The Swedish Labor Institute) 1979.

Annual report for the Directorate of Social Affairs for the year 1984, Ministry of Labor and Social Affairs, Bahrain, 1985.

Arab Gulf Program for UN Development Organizations (AGFUND), Reyadh, Saudi Arabia, 1984.

Assanah ath-thaneyah minal-khutta alkhmsyah (The second year of the 5-year-plan: an assessment), Ministry of Education, Department of Adult Education, Bahrain, June 1985. (Arabic)

Athar Al-Murabbeyat Al-Ajnabeyyat Ala Khas-is Al-Usrah Fil-Bahrain, 'Dirasah mydaneyyah' (Impact of foreign nannies on the characteristics of families in Bahrain), Ministry of Labor and Social Affairs, Bahrain, 1983. (Arabic)

Attaqreer A-Sanawi Lil-hy'ah Al-Ammah lit-Ta'meenat Al-Ijtima'eyyah/ 1983 (Annual report for Social Insurance Commission/1983), Bahrain, 1984. (Arabic)

Azhary, M. S. El. (Ed.), *The Impact of Oil Revenues on Arab Gulf Development*, Croom Helm, London & Sydney and Centre for Arab Gulf Studies, University of Exeter, the Petroleum Information Committee for the Arab Gulf States, 1984.

Az-zeera, Faheema. *Dour Markaz at-tadreeb al-mehani fi i'idad al-qwa al-Amela al-muwatena fi al-Bahrain* (The role of Vocational Training Center in training national manpower in Bahrain), The Arab Planning Institute, Kuwait, 1982. (Arabic)

Backgrounder: Literacy Education, UNESCO, Paris, June 1983.

Bahrain Census of Population and Housing – 1981, State of Bahrain, Cabinet Affairs, Directorate of Statistics, Nov. 1982.

Ball, Robert M., *Social Security, Today and Tomorrow*, New York: Columbia University Press, 1978.

Barsalou, Marie Judy, *Foreign Labor in Saudi Arabia: The Creation of Plural Society*, dissertation, Columbia University, 1985.

Baude, Amika, *Public Policy and Changing Family Patterns in Sweden, 1930–1977*, National Board of Health and Welfare, Stockholm, Sweden.

Beck, Lois and Kiddie, Nikki (Eds), *Women in the Muslim World*, Cambridge, Mass. and London: Harvard University Press, 1978.

Belsky, Jay, 'Infant Day Care: A Case for Concern?', *Bulletin of the Natural Center for Clinical Infant Programs*, vol. VI, no. 5 (Sept. 1986), p. 319.

Belsky, Jay and Steinberg, Laurence (1978), 'The Effects of Day Care: A Critical Review', *Child Development*, 49, pp. 229–949.

Bendix, Reinhard, 'Tradition and Modernity Reconsidered', *Comparative Studies in Society and History*, 9, 3 (1967) pp. 292–346.

Bently, William H., *Administering the Successful Vocational Education: A Guide for Administrators*, American Vocational Association, 1978.

Berfenstam, Ranger and William-Olsson, Inger, *Early Child Care in Sweden*, London: Gordon and Breach, 1979.

Birks, J. S. and Rimmer, J. A., *Developing Education Systems in the Oil States of Arabia: Conflicts of Purpose and Focus*, Occasional papers series No. 21, manpower and migration series No. 3, Centre for Middle Eastern and Islamic Studies, University of Durham, England, 1984, p. 5.

Birks, J. S. and Sinclair, C. A., *Arab Manpower*, London: Croom Helm, 1980.

Bishara, Abudulla, 'Majles Att-Awon Al-Khaleeji Wal-Wihdah Al-Arabiyah' (The GCC and Arab unity), *Al-Mustaqbal Al-Araby*, issue 79 (Sept. 1985). (Arabic)

Bishara, Abdulla, 'The Gulf Cooperation Council: Achievements and Challenges', *American Arab Affairs*, Washington, No. 7 (Winter 1983–84).

Boserup, Ester, *Women's Role in Economic Development*, New York: St. Martin's Press, 1970.

Bulloch, John, *The Gulf: A Portrait of Kuwait, Qatar, Bahrain and the UAE*, London: Century Publishing, 1984.

Carron, G. and Bordia, A. (Eds), *Issues in Planning and Implementing National Literacy Programs*, Paris: UNESCO, International Institute for Educational Planning, 1985.

Christian, Nancy, K. (Ed.), *Education in the 80's: Vocational Education*, Washington, D.C.: National Education Association Publication, 1982.

Clarke-Stewart, K. Alison and Fein, Greta G., 'Early childhood programs', in M. M. Maith and J. J. Campos (Eds), Ph. H. Mussen (Series Ed.), *Handbook of Child Psychology: Vol. 2 Infancy & Developmental Psychology*, New York: John Wiley.

Clerck, Marcel de, Where there's a will. . .', *The UNESCO Courier*, Feb. 1984, 37th year, Paris.

Cook, Alice H., Lorin, Val R. and Daniels, Arlene Kaplan (Eds), *Women and Trade Unions in Eleven Industrialized Countries*, Philadelphia: Temple University Press, 1984.

The Courier, 'Women: Tradition and Change, Paris: UNESCO, Apr. 1985.

Daleel Al-Mu-Assasat At-t'leemeyah Al-Khassa/1985–86 (Directory for private educational institutions for the year 1985–86), Ministry of Education, Bahrain, 1986. (Arabic)

Daleel Reyadh Al-Atfal/1983–84 (Directory of kindergartens for the year 1983–84), Ministry of Education, Bahrain, 1984. (Arabic)

David, Myriam and Lezine, Irene, *Early Child Care in France*, London: Gordon and Breach, 1975.

Day Care Survey 1970–71, Child Care Bulletin No. 7. Washington, D.C., 1971.

Dearden, Ann (Ed.), *Arab Women*, Report No. 27, revised 1983 ed, Minority Rights Group.

Demographic and Social Trends: Implications for Federal Support of Dependent-Care Services for Children and the Elderly, Select Committee on Children, Youth and Families, House of Representatives Ninety-Eight Congress, Dec. 1983.

Deutch, Karl, 'Social mobilization and political development', *The American Political Science Review*, vol. LV, no. 3 (Sept. 1961).

Dirasah an Awdha' Al-Mar'a fil-Usrah Al-Bahraineyyah, 'Dirasah Mydaneyyah' (A study on the condition of women and families in Bahrain), 'a field study'. An-Nahdhah Women Association, Bahrain, 1983. (Arabic)

Dirasah maidaneyah howla waqi' al-ummeyah bidowlatel-Bahrain (Women's illiteracy in Bahrain: a field study), An-Nahdah Association (forthcoming), 1983. (Arabic)

Dirasah Taq-yeemeyyah Limashrou' Al-Ra'idat Al-Mahaleyyat, 'Dirasah Mydaneyyah' (An assessment of local leaders program), 'a field study', Ministry of Labor and Social Affairs, Bahrain, 1983. (Arabic)

Ebrahim, Hassan ali Al-, *Kuwait and the Gulf, Small States and the International System*, Center for contemporary Arab Studies, Washington, D.C., London and Canberra: Croom Helm, 1984.

Ekistics, vol. 50, No. 330 (May 1983).

El-Azhari, M. S. (Ed.), *The Impact of Oil Revenues on Arab Gulf Development*, Center for Arab Gulf studies, University of Exeter, London & Sydney: Croom Helm, 1981.

Employment and Manpower Problems and Policy Issues in Arab Countries: Proposals for the Future, Geneva: ILO, 1983.

Fakhro, Munira, *Mahwe- Ummeyatel mar'a wttan- meyah ash-shamilah* (Adult education for women as part of an overall development). A paper presented to the training session for voluntary associations leaders, held in Bahrain, 27 Oct.–1 Nov. 1984. (Arabic)

Farjani, Nadir (Ed.), *Foreign Labor force in the Arab Gulf States*, Center for Arab Unity studies (Beirut), The Arab Institute for Planning (Kuwait), 1983. (Arabic)

Fernea, W. Elizabeth, *A Veiled Revolution: A Study Guide to the Film*, Austin, Texas, 1982, p. 6.

Financial Times, London, 4 Aug. 1985.

Foster-Carter, Aiden, 'From Rostow to Gunder Frank: Conflicting Paradigms in the Analysis of Underdevelopment', *World Development*, vol. 4, no. 3 (Mar. 1976) pp. 167–80.

Garland, Caroline and White, Stephanie, *Children and Day Nurseries, Management and Practice in Nine London Day Nurseries*, London: The High/Scope Press, 1980.

Gendt, Rein Van, *Return Migration and Reintegration Services*, Paris: Organization for European Cooperation & Development (OECD), 1977.

Grindle, Merilee (Ed.), *Politics and Policy Implementation in the Third World*, Princeton University Press, 1980.

Hatry, Harry, *Program Analysis for State and Local Governments*, The Urban Institute, 1976.

Herman, Alice and Komlosi, Sandor, *Early Child Care in Hungary*, London: Gordon and Breach, 1972.

Huntingdon, Samuel P., 'The change to Change: Modernization Development and Politics', *Comparative Politics, vol. 3* (1971) pp. 283–322.

Ibrahim, Saad Eddin, *The New Arab Social Order: A Study of Social Impact of Oil Wealth*, Westview special studies on the Middle East, Boulder, Col.: Westview Press; London: Croom Helm, 1982.

ILO and Women Workers: Activities in 1982–83, Report of the

International Labor Organization (ILO). E/CN.6/1984/5, 28 Nov. 1983, Vienna.

Industrial and Labor Relations Review (Apr. 1980).

Ispahani, Mahnaz Zahra, 'Alone Together: Regional Security Arrangements in Southern Africa and Arabian Gulf', *International Security*, vol. 8, no. 4 (Spring 1984).

Kahn, Alfred, *Studies in Social Policy and Planning*, New York: Russell Sage Foundation, 1969.

Kahn-Hut, Rachael, Daniels, Arlene Kaplan and Colvard, Richard, *Women and Work; Problems and Perspectives*, Oxford University Press, 1982.

Kamerman, Sheila B., *Parenting in an Unresponsive Society; Managing Work and Family*, New York: The Free Press, 1980.

Kamerman, Sheila B., *Child Care Programs in Nine Countries: A Report for the OECD Working Party on the Role of Women in the Economy*. OECD.

Kamerman, Sheila and Khan, Alfred (Eds), *Family Policy: Government and Families in Fourteen Countries*, New York: Columbia University Press, 1978.

Kamerman, Sheila and Kahn, Alfred, *Child Care, Family Benefits, and Working Parents: A Study in Comparative Policy*, New York: Columbia University Press, 1981.

Kessen, William (Ed.), *Childhood in China*, New Haven and London: Yale University Press, 1975.

Khalakdina, Margaret, *Early Child Care in India*, London: Gordon and Breach, 1979.

Khuri, Fuad I., *Tribe and State in Bahrain: The Transformation of Social and Political Authority in an Arab State*, Chicago and London: University of Chicago Press, 1980.

Kozol, Jonathan, *Illiterate America*, New York: Anchor Press/Doubleday Garden City, 1985.

Lall, Sanjaya, 'Is "dependence" a Useful Concept in Analysing Under-Development', *World Development*, 3, 11–12 (1975) pp. 799–810.

Lamar, Carl S. (Ed.), *Comprehensive Planning for Vocational Education: A Guide for Administrators*, American Vocational Association, 1978.

Leys, Colin, 'Underdevelopment and Dependency: Critical Notes', *Journal of contemporary Asia*, 7, 1 (1977) pp. 92–107.

Luscher, Kurt K., Ritter, Verena and Gross, Peter, *Early Childhood Care in Switzerland*, London: Gordon and Breach, 1973.

Mahler, Vincent A., *Dependency Approaches to International Political Economy: A Cross-national Study*, New York: Columbia University Press, 1980.

Mernissi, Fatima, *Beyond the Veil: Male–Female Dynamics in a Modern*

Moslem Society, New York, London, Sydney and Toronto: Schenkman Publishing Company, Halsted Press Division, John Wiley and Sons, 1975.
MERIP Reports (Middle East and Information Projects), No. 132, New York (May 1985).
Middle East Economic Digest, 27 (34), (26 Aug. 1983).
Middle East Economic Survey, 26 (24), (28 Mar. 1983).
The Middle East Magazine, Ashford, England, No. 120 (Oct. 1984).
The Middle East Magazine, 'Why Kuwaiti Women Want the Right to Vote', London, Oct. 1985.
The Middle East Review, 1985, World Almanac Publications, England, 1985.
Mideast Markets, 11 (17), (20 Aug. 1984).
Mubayedh, Mamdooh Al and Jishi, Baheya Al, *Taqweem Awdha' Door Al-Hadhana wa Reuadh Al-Atfal Al-Wataneya fil Bahrain, dirasa Mydaneya* (Assessing child care services, a field study), The High Council for Youth and Sports, and the UNICEF, 1980. (Arabic).
Maddison, John, *Radio and Television in Literacy*, A survey of the use of the broadcasting media in combatting illiteracy among adults, Paris: UNESCO, 1971.
Massialas, Byron G. and Mikati, Jamila F., *Strategies for Educating Arab Women to Participate in National Development*, Paper presented to the Regional Conference on 'planning for Arab women's economic participation', sponsored by the Institute for Women's Studies in the Arab World, Beirut University College, Nicosia, Cyprus, 24–30 June 1985.
Mattar, Aishah, *Dowrel Jam-ieyat attataw-o-ieyah fi harakat mahwel-ummeyah bidowal al-khaleej* (The role of voluntary organizations in literacy campaign in the Gulf States), Paper presented to the training session for voluntary association leaders, held in Bahrain in 27 Oct.–1 Nov. 1984. (Arabic)
Myers, Robert G., *Programming for Early Childhood Care and Development: Complementary Approaches and Program Options*, Chapter V, produced for UNICEF field manual, 1986.
Myrdal, Alva, *Nation and family*, Cambridge, Mass. and London: The MIT Press, 1968.
Nakhleh, Emile, *Bahrain: Political Development in a Modernizing Society*, Mass.: Lexington Books, 1976.
Nuget, Jeffrey B. and Thomas, Theodor H. (Eds), *Bahrain and the Gulf: Past Perspectives and Alternative Futures*, London and Sydney: Croom Helm, 1985.
The New York Times, 16 Mar. 1986, p. 33.
The New York Times, section 12, 13 Apr. 1986, pp. 24–30.
Niblock, Tim (Ed.), *Social and Economic Development in the Arab*

Gulf, London: Croom Helm; New York: St. Martin's Press, 1980.

Obaid, Thoraya, *Dowr Al-Munadhdhgamat An-Nisa'eyyagh Fi Majal Mahwel-Ummeyyah* (The role of women's organization in the Arab world in eradicating illiteracy), a study presented at a seminar held in Damascus, Syria, 6–10 Jan. 1985. (Arabic)

Orbis, Autumn 1984.

The Operational Seminar: A Pioneering Method of Trading for Development, Educational studies and documents, UNESCO, 20 Nov. 1976.

Pizzo, Peggy Daly, *The Infant Day Care Debate: Not Whether But How*, Day care and development council of America, Washington, D.C.

Preliminary Investigation into the Social Situation and Needs of Women in Villages in Bahrain, United Nations Development Program (UNDP), DP/UN/Bah-73-009/1 Bahrain, UN, New York, 1977.

Pressman, J. L. and Wildavsky, A., *Implementation*, Berkeley, Los Angeles, London: University of California Press, 1973.

Pringle, Mia Kellmer and Naidoo, Sanhya, *Early Child Care In Britain*, London: Gordon and Breach, 1975.

Pye, Lucien, 'The Concept of Political Development', in Finkle and Gable (Eds), *Political Development and Social Change*, 2nd Edn, New York: John Wiley, 1971.

Ramazani, Nesta, 'Arab Women in the Gulf', *The Middle East Journal*, vol. 39, no. 2 (Spring 1985).

Regional Plan of Action for the Integration of Women in Development in Western Asia, Economic Commission for Western Asia (ECWA), 1978.

Rumaihi, M. G., *Bahrain: Social and Political Change since the First World War*, London and New York: Bowker, 1976.

Rumaihi, M. G., *Beyond Oil: Unity and Development in the Gulf*, London: Al-Saqi Books, 1986.

Rumaihi, M. G. Al-, *Al-Khaleej Lysa naftan: Dirasah fi Ishkalyati Attanmeyah wal-wahdah*, (The Gulf is not oil only: a study on the dilemma of development and unity), Kuwait: Kadhmah Publishing, 1983. (Arabic)

Rumaihi, M. G. Al, *The expected social and psychological impact on the Arab World of the fall in oil prices*, Paper presented to the symposium on 'Arabs without oil', organized by: Arab Research Centre, London, 25–26 June, 1985.

Robinson, Halbert B., Robinson, Nancy M., Walins, Martin, Bronfenbrenner, Urie and Richmond, Julius, B., *Early Child Care in the United States of America*, London: Gordon and Breach, 1973.

Robinson, Nancy M., Robinson, Halburn, B., Darling, Martha and Holm, Gretchen, *A World of Children, Day Care and Preschool Institutions*, Monterey, Calif.: Brooks/Cole Publishing Co., 1979.

Saadawi, Nawal, *The Hidden Face of Eve: Women in the Arab World*, translated and edited by Dr Sherif Hetata, Boston: Beacon Press, 1980.

Sabra, Yahya M., *The Impact of the Saudi–Bahrain Causeway on Trade in Bahrain*, Bahrain, 1985. (Arabic)

Safran, Nadav, *Saudi Arabia: The Ceaseless Quest for Security*, Cambridge, Mass. and London: The Belknap Press of Harvard Univerity Press, 1985.

Seccombe, Ian J., *International Labor Migration and Skill Scarcity in the Hashemite Kingdom of Jordan*, Geneva: ILO, 1984.

Seccombe, Ian J., 'Labor Migration to the Arabian Gulf: Evolution and Characteristics 1929–1950', *British Society for Middle East Bulletin*, 10 (1), (1983).

Serageldin, Ismael, Socknat, A. James, Birks, Stace, Li, Bob and Sinclair, Clive A., *Manpower and International Labor Migration in the Middle East and North Africa*. (A World Bank publication), Oxford University Press, 1983.

Seznec, Jean-Francois, *The Financial Markets of the Arabian Gulf: Bahrain, Kuwait, Saudi Arabia* (Forthcoming), London: Croom Helm, 1987.

Shaw, R. Paul, *Mobilizing Human Resources in the Arab World*, London: KPI, 1983.

Sheffield, James R. and Diejomaoh, Victor P. *Non-Formal Education in African Development*, New York: African American Institute, 1972.

Sirriyeh, Hussein, *US Policy in the Gulf 1968–77: Aftermath of the British Withdrawal*, London: Ithaca Press, 1984.

Smith, Ralph E. (Ed.), *The Subtle Revolution: Women at Work*, Washington, D.C.: The Urban Institute, 1979.

Smith, Tony, 'The Underdevelopment of Development Literature: the Case of Dependency Theory', *World Politics*, vol. XXXI, no. 1 (Oct. 1978) pp. 247–88.

Social Indicators for Bahrain. Ministry of Labor and Social Affairs, Bahrain, Dec. 1982.

Soffan, Linda, *The Women of the United Arab Emirates*, London: Croom Helm, 1980.

Statistical Abstracts 1983, Bahrain Council of Ministers, Central Statistics Organizations, Dec. 1984.

Statistical Abstracts 1984, Council of Ministers, Central Statistics Organization, Bahrain, Dec. 1985.

The Sunday Times Magazine, London, 10 Nov. 1985, pp. 65–85.

Time Magazine, 6 Feb. and 30 Apr. 1984.

Toward a National Policy for Children and Families. Washington, D.C.: National Academy of Sciences, 1976.

Training Statistics, 1982–1984. Ministry of Labor and Social Affairs,

Directorate of Manpower Development, Planning and Evaluation Section, Bahrain, 1985.
UNESCO, *The Needs of Asia in Primary Education*, Educational studies and documents, No. 41, 1961.
Vocational Training Systems in Member States of European Community: Comparative study, CCEDEFOP guide, Berlin: European Centre for the development of vocational training CEDEFOP, 1984.
Werker, Scot, 'Beyond the Dependency Paradigm', *Journal of Contemporary Asia*, 15 (1985) pp. 79–95.
Wistrand, Brigitta, *Swedish Women on the Move* The Swedish Institute, 1981.
Youssef, Nadia, 'Education and Female Modernism in the Muslim World', *Journal of International Affairs*, vol. 30, no. 2 (1976–77) pp. 191–209.
Youssef, Nadia, *Women and Work in Developing Societies*, Institute of International Studies, University of California, Berkeley, population monograph series, no. 15, 1974.
Zuraiqat, Sami, *Khuttat Tadreeb Ashrat Ala-ph Bahraini fi Sanateha al-thalitha: Ardh wa taqyeem* (Training plan for 10,000 Bahraini in its third year: an assessment), Bahrain Centre for Studies & Research, Bahrain, 1983. (Arabic)

Index